BEES IN SOME BONNETS

BEES IN SOME BONNETS

Lord Mancroft

Bachman and Turner, London

Bachman & Turner Ltd.
The Old Hop Exchange
1/3 Central Buildings
24 Southwark Street,
London S.E.1.

First published 1979

ISBN 0 85974 088 9 Casebound

Typeset by Inforum Ltd., Portsmouth
Printed in Great Britain by Hollen Street Press Ltd., Slough
Bound by J. M. Dent & Sons Ltd., Letchworth

Contents

Acknowledgment

Many of the following pieces have appeared in the pages of *Punch*. I am grateful to the present Editor, Mr. Alan Coren, for permission to include them in this book.

My two previous books *Booking the Cooks* and *A Chinaman in my Bath* also consisted largely of pieces that had originally appeared in *Punch*. Since both those books are now out of print, I have taken the opportunity to reproduce within the pages of this book a few of the less ephemeral pieces that appeared in the other two.

Dedication

To my Children
Victoria, Jessica and Benjamin without whose critical
examination and well-intentioned comment this book
would have been much easier to write.

1

Bees, Bats and Windmills

Pottiness, of course, is largely a matter of degree. At the harmless end of the scale we find our Miss Mustow who lives a few doors down from the *Rising Sun*. We had long noticed that she always bowed when the name of the Devil was mentioned in Church. Eventually, the vicar plucked up courage and asked her why this was. "Well, Vicar," she said, "politeness costs nothing and you never know when it may not come in useful."

At the other end of the scale were the Bedlams, the lunatic asylums of the eighteenth century, where poor demented creatures were stripped naked and flogged whilst handsome ladies of fashion came to watch, much as you and I might go to the Zoo or Madame Tussauds.

In between the two extremes lies a fascinating grey area where belfries are full of bats, Don Quixote tilts at windmills mistaking them for giants, and Squire Mytton sets fire to his night-shirt to scare away the hiccups.

But a bee in your bonnet is different. You may be to all intents perfectly normal and yet have some little quirk or crank, some pet aversion of your own. Lord Melbourne, as well as the Duke of Wellington, thought that all new legislation, however desirable, was to be deplored, and Sir Frederick Banbury went so far as to oppose every bill that was brought before Parliament whilst he was a member.

Our own Mr. William Hamilton MP has a bee in his bonnet about the Royal Family. Mr. Gladstone used to pray with prostitutes and could not understand why this practice raised the eyebrows of even his most loyal supporters. And only recently have we learned that the late

1

Mr. Mackenzie King, the distinguished Canadian Prime Minister, used to commune regularly with the spirit of his long dead cocker-spaniel.

Eddie Devonshire, the 10th Duke, had a bee in his bonnet about the Cloth and firmly maintained that behind every absurdity or undesirable piece of nonsense you were bound to find a clergyman. His Grace could not understand why there was such a sharp reaction from the Bishop's benches when he was rash enough to advance this theory during a debate on education in the Lords.

My Uncle Henry always insisted that *The Times* be ironed before it was brought to him of a morning. So would I, were it not for the fact that even if *The Times* were obtainable in our part of Gloucestershire, I myself should have to do both the bringing and the ironing. In all other respects, however, I am glad to think that I am perfectly normal.

At least, that was my thinking until I once casually advanced it to my old friend Alan Herbert – the incomparable APH. We were strolling together along the Embankment one warm Wednesday afternoon after lunching in the offices of *Punch,* to which he was a major and regular contributor and I a minor and irregular one.

He stopped and stared at me in horror. "Perfectly normal," he said, "But you can't be. Nobody's perfectly normal so if you really are perfectly normal you must be unique and therefore wildly abnormal." It took me some time to work this out.

It would have taken a barrack-room let alone a bonnet to house all APH's bees. I suppose his finest bee was not a bee at all but a cow, the famous negotiable cow. APH objected to writing cheques on the orthodox cheque form. On one occasion he wrote out a cheque for his income tax on the stomach of a cow, stuck a stamp on its horn and led it down to Somerset House.

This event occurred originally as fiction in one of his splendid "Misleading Cases" but on his 80th birthday,

Punch remounted the whole saga in the flesh and a very fine crowd it attracted too.

APH did not confine his cheque-writing to bovine circles. He wrote cheques on such things as the tails of shirts and on biscuits. I once lent him some small change for a taxi fare home after dining in the Temple and he wrote me a cheque in verse on the label of a bottle of claret. It begins "Pay Stormont Mancroft, (best of men), the princely sum of two pounds ten."

Eventually the bank got fed up with all this and insisted that in future he should write his cheques only on their recognised cheque forms. APH duly complied but always wrote the cheque on the back of the form rather than the front. Coutts wisely threw in the towel and APH returned to his task of improving our divorce laws and civilizing the river Thames.

But back to the Embankment. Alan and I strolled on towards Westminster in the autumn sunshine. He asked me what the Lords were discussing that afternoon. I told him (and I am speaking from memory) that the first item on the Order Paper was the Aberdeen Harbour (Sludge Removal and Disposal) Confirmation Order Bill and I felt I personally couldn't do much good about that one.

He stopped me again. "Never try and do good," he said. "If you want to make your mark in the public weal, don't waste time trying to do good. Just try and stop less intelligent people than yourself from trying *their* hands at doing good. Political do-gooders usually wreak great harm." (I presumed we must overlook divorce and the river Thames). He patted my shoulder affectionately and stumped down the steps to catch a launch back to Hammersmith. A splendid man. When he died, all our serious newspapers accorded him and his bees a leading article as well as the usual obituary notice – a rare but richly deserved tribute. I often wonder why he was never made a Peer. He would have been in his element.

He had, however, given my conscience a jerk. Had

any of my own bees (some of which can be found buzzing in the following pages) flown over into the realms of needless do-gooding? Equally, I wish I had been more widely awake when they passed laws like the one that makes it compulsory to advertise for a nightwatch-person rather than a nightwatchman and having found such a paragon, you discover that another law now makes it practically impossible to sack anybody even if he or she goes to sleep on the job or invites the burglars in. That's the trouble with do-gooders – give them an inch (sorry, 25 millimetres) and they'll take an ell.

There is one thing, however, that has begun to worry me and I ought to have asked APH for his views. The bee is an elegant sagacious and industrious creature. Would it not be more appropriate to talk about people having human beings in their bonnets rather than bees?

2
Pet aversions

Gilbert Harding used to work himself into a rage if he was offered margarine instead of butter. It was this preoccupation with trivialities, they said, that detracted from the roll of his thunder. He should have aimed at more important targets.

I snarl, as you do, at the man who bangs me on the back and calls me by the wrong christian name. If tolerating bad manners be the test of good ones then I must start with names. I wish I could be more tolerant of the mishandling of names. I suppose I have no right to object if some pimply page minces through the lounge of the *Grand Babylon*, bawling out my name above the sound of Musak. I wish, too, that I did not want to strangle the name dropper. "As Enoch was saying only yesterday," or "Quintin told me this himself, but in strict confidence, of course."

The name-dropper is always with us but the political specimen is more tiresome than most because it so often turns out that he really is on those terms with Mr. Powell and Lord Hailsham. That only makes it worse.

The Press encourages the mishandling of names with its Cliff this and Margaret that and Tony the other. If Betty Brown marries John Smith I thought she became Mrs. John Smith. But no. Nowadays she appears as Mrs. Betty Smith with her age in brackets, whether this be relevant to the news or not. Of course, if John Smith becomes a peer we move into lusher and more fancy fields. Not only will his age, probable or improbable income, and all his christian names be recited in full, but his name will be followed by his family motto. This often proves to be embarrassingly inappropriate. If Lord Smith has the misfortune to be charged with driving on the wrong side of the road at two o'clock in the morning, then his family motto will prove to be "safe and sure". And if he is making a third and particularly bizarre appearance in the divorce courts then it's a guinea to a gooseberry his motto will be "faithful unto death".

I suppose, however, that it is on the telephone that our personal behaviour is put to the sharpest test. "Is that Mr. Smith? One moment please, I have a call for you." Dead silence for thirty seconds. Then another and even more impersonal female voice, "Oh, good morning, Mr. Smith, Mr. Splurdge is calling you." "Then put Splurdge on." More silence because the accursed Splurdge has forgotten he's told his secretary to get Mr. Smith on the line and has wandered off next door to tell the sales director his newest dirty story. (Splurdge, by the way, is always photographed in the act of telephoning. That's to show he's important). Other than replacing your receiver there is no easy cure for this particular discourtesy because it's all wrapped up in secretarial one-upmanship. Splurdge's secretary isn't going to have her man waste a second of his time waiting for me to come on the line, nor, vice versa (and bless her little heart), is yours.

Of course, if Splurdge does condescend to ring me up personally, he will announce himself as Jim (as if I know no other Jims) and he will do it at home and it will be either when I am in the bath or in the middle of dinner. Some sixth sense tells him how to judge the moment to a nicety. His sixth sense is acute. It is the other five that are deficient. My father had a useful formula for this sort of pest. "Tell Mr. Splurdge," he would say, "that if he wishes to do something for me I will leave my *sole dieppoise* and come to the telephone. If, on the other hand, he wishes me to do something for him, will he please write and tell me what it is?" That usually puts paid to Mr. Splurdge but, alas, I haven't my father's courage. Anyhow; even if Splurdge does write, he'll probably fall into another category of aversion, the proud possessor of the illegible signature. This is not only bad manners but unpardonable conceit. You can best retaliate by cutting out the signature and pasting it on your envelope in return.

I once had the misfortune to serve on the staff of a general whose signature looked like a street map of Wolverhampton. I could usually decipher his handwriting after a time-wasting struggle, but on one occasion he wrote in the margin of a very important document what appeared to be the word "concubine".

"Sir," I asked (always the conscientious officer) "why have you written the word 'concubine' against this item recording the views of the Chiefs of Staff on the possible use of detachable pontoons at Chittagong?" He peered angrily at the spidery deposit and said, "That word isn't concubine. It isn't a word at all. I had just refilled my fountain-pen and was testing it to see that the ink ran smoothly." He ended his war, I'm glad to say, as Garrison Commander, Reykjavik.

I have now successfully prevented Splurdge from telephoning (not, you will note, 'phoning) or writing to me, but here he is, by golly, at the front door. Splurdge is the kind of man you like better the more you see him less. He is, of course, late. His handshake is wet and clinging. He comes in, bouncing apologies in front of him, and expatiating on the state of the London traffic. He goes backwards and forwards over this like an old woman darning a sock, as if he and nobody else had ever had it so bad. (I myself am a punctual person but I find that my punctuality makes me very lonely).

He asks if he may use my telephone. He may, and does – at length. He needs, he tells me, a drink. I was actually going to offer him one. He asks for a Bloody Mary. Vodka is the one thing we haven't got in the house. It would be. The Splurdges of this world always ask for something we don't happen to have. He puts up with second best. Graciously, he drinks our health.

(Cheers! Bungers! Down the hatch, or worse). He then puts the glass down on the best piece of furniture in the room. It leaves an obscene little ring which we shall not discover until it is too late to obliterate the damage. He takes from his too well cut suit a too well engine-turned cigarette case and offers us one of his own brand – specially made for me at Dunhill's, old boy, only two guineas a box. Why do the Splurdges of this world always operate in guineas? Why does Splurdge assume that I have no cigarettes in the house and even if I have, that I don't know the right moment to offer them? The trouble is that I probably haven't and, not smoking them myself, probably don't. He drops the stub on the carpet and thoughtfully grinds it in.

Oh yes, and his dog. I'd forgotten that infernal Toto. Although the animal lobby is politically amongst the most tiresome and unscrupulous, I've nothing particularly against dogs, only their owners. Most dog owners, at least in London, lose all sense of decency. They certainly lose all sense of smell; Toto gambols round our feet, swishing the Famille Rose off the table with his unhygienic bottle-brush of a tail, sabotaging all rational conversation with his persistent yaps encouraged by "There's a good boy – good dog, Toto." Splurdge loves Toto for his advertisement value, but Toto strikes me as ambassador and envoy plenipotentiary from the Farnham Sewage Works.

But Splurdge isn't really interested in me, he's only interested in Splurdge. That's the real basis of so many pet aversions. The word "you" doesn't enter Splurdge's vocabulary. He doesn't ask how I do and if he does he interrupts me and bears down upon me to talk about his lumbago, his girl at Heathfield (brilliant – sleeps in the bed in which Princess Alexandra slept), his useful coup with Norcross, his new Jaguar – sorry, Jag.

I bet that Jaguar's got a name. "Jenny the Jag" or "The Bomb".

My neighbour once had three Aberdeens named Tom, Dick and Harry. That was pardonable and is at

8

least to be preferred to the pomposity with which pedigree bulls are christened. Fancy having to answer to the name of Entwistle Grand Trumpeter the Third. But cars just mustn't have names.

Nor must the Splurdges of this world park them permanently outside my house. I know all that stuff about the Queen's highway and know I have no more right to park my car in Eaton Square than I have to park a grand piano. But I resent the commuters from the canasta belt whose beastly cars block my front door daily from nine till five.

Last week I received a ticket for parking my car outside my own home in Chelsea. The warden, like the keeper at Blackpool Zoo, was quite nice about it, and when I asked where might be the nearest place I could park without running foul of the law, he replied, after some thought, that he felt it must be Gatwick Airport.

Another of my neighbours noticed that it was the same car parked every day outside his house. He dealt promptly with his particular Splurdge. He put a match-stick into the lock of the car door and chopped it off flush. When Splurdge returned and inserted the key, he drove the match deep into the mechanism of the lock and it took Messrs Car Mart and their merry men two days to get the door off and on again.

This is effective, but of doubtful legality.

It is also bad luck on Mrs. Splurdge for whom I am beginning to feel a little sorry. She leads a rotten life. Splurdge is, of course, wildly unfaithful with what he undoubtedly refers to as little "bits".

Adultery, however, can hardly be classed as a pet aversion so perhaps we had better confer the benefit of the doubt. His household behaviour is tiresome enough even without that benefit.

He snores; he never remembers to shut the door; he never puts the cap back on the toothpaste. He leaves a newspaper looking as if he had read it behind an aeroplane propellor. He cuts bits out before Mrs. Splurdge has had a chance to read it. There's no greater test of mental control than picking up a newspaper that contains a hole without wondering what it is that has been cut out.

However, I expect she gets her own back by calling him Hubby.

I am trivial. I make much ado about next to nothing. I am sorry. But I am on the late Gilbert Harding's side, butter, margarine and all. It is the smallest of aversions that does the greatest damage. It is the little car chugging along safely in the middle of the M1 at twenty-nine and a half miles per hour that exasperates us into disaster; not old Splurdge in his Jag.

Beethoven the great, the celestial Beethoven, wrote a piece called, *Rage over a lost penny*. He was right.

3
Made in Heaven

Lady Wootton is always threatening to abolish the House of Lords though I believe that, secretly, she's quite fond of us and we're certainly very fond of her. And she's now demonstrated that she's as brave as she is charming. Believe it or not, she's trying to amend the Marriage Laws and that not only requires courage, it requires infinite patience. Here I know what I'm talking about because I once tried to do it myself and it took me eleven years to get my little Bill onto the Statute Book. But this, of course, was before I had received Alan Herbert's caution about the dangers of trying to do good.

Oddly enough, my Bill bore the same name as Lady Wootton's – Marriage (Enabling) Bill. Mine, however, was much more limited in its scope than hers. All I wanted to do was to make it possible for you to marry your divorced wife's sister but Lady W. wants to upset the whole Table of Kindred and Affinity which you will find at the back of the Book of Common Prayer. This, you will remember, is the bit you turned to during the less exhilarating passages of the sermon in school chapel and wondered why you weren't allowed to marry your grandmother's sister's niece as if you could recognise the girl when you ran into her in the street. There's a lot more in this vein – your uncle's daughter, and your step-father's mother and so on. I'm sure there's some sound theological reasoning behind all this though much of it escapes me and, indeed, Lady Wootton too, because she wants to give the whole lot the heave-ho. I've warned her, however, she's in for trouble if she wants to tamper with the rules of matrimony. Church

11

and State will rise against her in wrath as they did against me and I only wanted to make one tiny change, namely, the one about your divorced wife's sister whilst leaving your grannie's sister, niece and all the others strictly in *locus quo*.

Perhaps I'd better explain in more detail what it was I was trying to achieve because I don't want to be accused of giving house-room to improper bees in my bonnet.

What happened was this. There was a chap in my regiment whom we'll call Sgt. Robinson for the very good reason that it happened to be his name and I have his permission to use his name and his story, too. He was stationed at GHQ Cairo in the earlier part of the war where he met, fell in love with, and in due course married a girl in the ATS who worked on one of the GHQ switchboards. With the arrival on the scene of Rommel, most of the girls, including Mrs. Robinson who was by then expecting a baby, were evacuated down to the Cape, and eventually back to England. In Mrs. Robinson's case it happened to be Scotland and in due course she landed up with her unmarried sister Dorothy in Dumfries. Three months later little Jennifer Robinson joined them. Unfortunately, Mrs. Robinson had an eye for the boys, particularly if they were serving in the Polish Air Force, and with one such boy she eventually decamped leaving little Jennifer in a reluctant Auntie's care.

Sgt. Robinson soon got to hear of all this, applied for and was granted compassionate leave, and came home to meet his new daughter and new sister-in-law for the first time. He also met his wife who told him that she wished to marry her Polish friend and could she please have her freedom. The divorce went through in due course and Robinson was given custody of his little girl. Not unnaturally, (since he had been transferred home to England), he began to see a lot of the sister-in-law who was caring for his child and eventually the inevitable happened. They fell in love and decided to get married. But could they? Oh, indeed no, because although such a

12

marriage might have seemed to an impartial observer eminently sensible, such observer might well, as Sgt. Robinson had done, have overlooked the Table of Kindred and Affinity, and this specifically forbade their union.

Here let me interrupt myself to make certain there's no confusion between Divorced Wife's sister and Deceased Wife's sister. The second girl's in order and has been since 1911 though goodness knows she, too, caused enough trouble in her day. Have a look at the Peers' Chorus in *Iolanthe* – "and try to prick that annual blister – marriage with deceased wife's sister."

No, it was Divorced Wife's sister that had tripped up Sgt. Robinson, and when he came to ask my advice I had to admit to my shame that I'd overlooked it too. (Rubbish! I hadn't overlooked it at all. I never even knew about it.)

Well, there was only one thing to be done and that was what I did. I consulted learned friends at the Chancery Bar (where I was trying to earn a living) and we duly drafted my Marriage (Enabling) Bill. It had a mixed reception. A lot of Bishops came down to the House of Lords and said that a vote for Mancroft would be a vote for incest. This, I argued, was putting an unduly strict interpretation on Leviticus XXv.21 which was written for the guidance of a primitive people living in the desert about 5000 years ago. (The next chapter of Leviticus, for instance, is much concerned with matters like priests making bald patches on their heads as a sign of mourning.)

I also discovered the existence of what might be called a Divorced Wife's Sisters' Club. It wasn't a big Club but if everybody who was involved took the trouble (as I believe they did) to write to me when the Bill was going through Parliament, I should imagine that about 150 couples were able to get married when my Bill eventually became law. (Tom and Dorothy Robinson asked me to be best man at their wedding which I thought was touching.)

Not everybody was so kindly disposed. One lady, for instance, wrote to me from Manchester saying that she had been living with her brother-in-law for nearly twenty five years in what she and he imagined to be Holy Wedlock. The Union had not been happy and when he read the news about my Bill and realised that he wasn't married at all, he heaved a sigh of relief, folded his newspaper, and went to live with a bar-maid in Bridlington.

My chief opponent was, of course, the Archbishop of Canterbury – Archbishop Geoffrey Fisher whom I held in high regard. There were some who thought him pompous and self-important. Well, a triple-first does not encourage mock modesty, but he was well aware of his limitations. He admitted cheerfully that he looked too prim and had too much of the school ma'am in his make-up, and I heard him say more than once how much he regretted that he had never seen service in some rough industrial parish.

But throughout all our negotiations I found him to be a likeable and warm-hearted man. Thoughtful, too. He always offered me a large glass of sherry at the end of our meetings, having previously told his chaplain to find out what sort of sherry I preferred.

His chaplain was an excellent man and his talents extended beyond the realms of the sherry cupboard. I'm a great one for striking whilst the iron is hot and the chaplain discovered this and, though never forgetting where his first loyalties lay, he usually managed to let me know in advance what the temperature was in the archiepiscopal ironing-room.

My happiest encounter with him was really a non-existent encounter. I rang him up one morning to ask for an appointment with Dr. Fisher, and instead of hearing the chaplain's usual cheerful boom, I found myself listening to a sweet and seductive female voice. "Oh dear," I said, "I'm afraid I must have got a wrong number. Is that the Archbishop of Canterbury's office?" A startled note crept in between those of sweetness and

14

seduction. "Archbishop of Canterbury!" she exclaimed, "Anything but!" The Archbishop, when we told him, was delighted.

Now the basis of the Archbishop's opposition was simple. Most of the problems with which I was concerned were likely to arise in crowded, working-class households where the presence of an attractive sister-in-law might prove a disturbing temptation if marriage was an ultimate possibility. It could be argued in return, I would have thought, that if a man knew he could never be made to marry the girl he might be even more tempted to misbehave himself. My old friend, Lord Goschen, went off on a different tack and argued in debate that adultery was not the prerogative of the working-class. There was, he maintained, more family adultery in the House of Lords than anywhere else, with the possible exception of the Household Cavalry. This proposition, though interesting, did little for my cause though I can hardly go so far as to blame it for the loss of my Bill.

For the next seven years, I was otherwise employed in various Government appointments but eventually, at the behest of my Bank Manager, I returned to the Back Benches and also to my Marriage (Enabling) Bill. The Bishops on this occasion were prepared to overlook Leviticus. The Archbishop was concerned with more important affairs of state and my little Bill slipped quietly through one wet Thursday afternoon when nobody was looking. On an even wetter Friday afternoon, my good friend, Sir Gerald Wills, MP for Bridgewater, managed to wiggle it through the Commons without anybody objecting there either, which is a procedure Lady Wootton will find much more difficult now than it was in those days. Nevertheless, there we were, home and dry.

Tom and Dorothy Robinson were married in a dreary suburban Register Office. They would have liked to have been married in church, since both took their religion seriously and neither of them had been what is quaintly called the guilty party.

But no, this is not allowed. There are admittedly some clergymen, more broad-minded than others, who will conduct a service of blessing after a marriage in a Register Office where the parties, like Tom and Dorothy, are innocent of any scandalous behaviour. This custom is becoming more common and is obviously better than nothing. You can even occasionally find (as the Duke of Windsor did) a clergyman actually prepared to marry in church a person who has been through the divorce courts. I believe it will not be long before we shall have to have a rethink about the whole question of remarriage after divorce. In the meantime we have to put up with a ceremony in the Register Office, and some of these take a bit of putting up with, too. It's a woefully arid and unromantic little affair.

Tom and Dorothy were married in an office that would have made a British Rail waiting room look like Canterbury Cathedral by comparison. The ceremony was certainly swift and sure but it had all the glamour and warmth of the Pay Parades we used to go through in the Army.

Flushed with the success of my Marriage (Enabling) Bill I rashly mentioned this new matter one evening on "Any Questions". I asked whether something couldn't be done to give the Register Office ceremony a little more Pomp and Circumstance and throw a stronger light on the importance of marriage and the marriage promises. I should have known better. The Institute of Population Registration (no less) set about organising an enquiry into how the Civil Marriage Ceremony could be improved and it appointed me to be one of the enquirers.

Now the law governing the Civil Marriage Ceremony happens to be short and sensible. It is contained in the Act of 1949 which says that all that is required is this simple form of words – "I do solemnly declare that I know not of any lawful impediment why I, John Smith, may not be joined in matrimony to Mary Brown. I call upon these persons here present to witness that I do take thee, Mary Brown, to be my lawful wedded wife," and, hey presto, that's it. Mary, thou art now Mrs. John Smith, whether thou hast spotted it or not. There are, of course, some attendant formalities, such as establishing identify, signing the register, issuing certificates, and the handing over of some money. How the rest of the ceremony proceeds depends upon local custom, the whim of the Registrar, and the wishes of the parties concerned. Registrars, we learned, earn a maximum of £3,000 per annum and their Society has recently considered striking for more. And Communists, we discovered, favour St. Pancras Town Hall for their nuptials.

Naturally, we found widespread variations and, to do them justice, the Registrar General and the local authorities have already been putting their heads together to try and bring some order out of chaos. The local authorities come into it because they have to provide the accommodation. Some authorities are more generous in this respect than others, but whether their wedding party numbers only a dozen, or looks like becoming a huge and fashionable mob, the room should be pleasant and dignified, and provided with decent cloakroom facilities and a good-sized ante-room or marshalling yard.

One difficulty is that so many people want to get married on a Saturday. This causes traffic jams in the Registrar's marshalling yard, and worse jams in the car park. Woe betide any party who's late, and if the bridegroom fails to turn up (which happens surprisingly often) the bride's next-of-kin may have a very stroppy Registrar on their hands.

Problems do not end here. Flowers? Yes, but there'll be a row if half a dozen couples all sniff appreciatively at the same floral arrangement on the same morning, and discover later that they've all got the whole of the same bill.

Music? I would have thought not, if only because the civil ceremony must in no way assume a religious mien, and music introduces an element of risk. Besides, if couple A wants the wedding march from *Lohengrin*, and couple B wants *Beat me Brother with a Solid Four*, there'll have to be some pretty slick changing of cassettes on a busy Saturday.

A ring? Yes, because this introduces an element of pledge and permanence. Two rings? Maybe, but one class-conscious Registrar informed us that no English gentleman ever wears a wedding ring. Photography? Yes, but not during the ceremony or the signing of the register.

The local authority do admittedly give the Registrar a £100 clothing grant but I think they ought to go further and provide a robe adaptable for a fat or a thin Registrar or Registress. They do this in France, where the civil ceremony is invariably performed by the Mayor – something which would send most of our Mayors up the wall.

In Scotland, as in America, you can be married (with suitable licence) in a private house. Why not in England?

We must draft some appropriate words of congratulation and encouragement with which the Registrar can conclude the ceremony, so as to impress everybody with the importance of what has happened. These words should be standard, and not left to the Registrar. Unfortunately (and I think this is sad), there can be no suggestion that the union be blessed, because the ceremony must be strictly non-religious. "Do you mean to say that if I were to sneeze while I'm signing the register you couldn't even say God bless you?" I asked our local Registrar as I was paying my fees the day before my own wedding. He looked at me coldly, and went on counting out my change.

4

Hitler disappoints

I only heard Hitler speak once and that was entirely by accident. At the time (it was the spring of 1932) I was an extra-mural student at Bonn University. The authorities used to allow a few foreigners like myself to attend courses in special subjects without actually enrolling as full-blown undergraduate members of the University. I had signed on for the short music degree, a degree which, to nobody's surprise, I failed to obtain by almost the largest margin of marks in the history of the Music School at Bonn.

While at Winchester I had, thanks to the misguided encouragement of the late Sir George Dyson, taken up the 'cello. I didn't actually put it down until I was demobilised in 1946. I then made a careful appreciation of the situation and decided that you cannot play the 'cello slightly. You either play it or you don't. So, to the understandable relief of my friends and relations, I put it down.

No such misgivings clouded my judgment in Bonn during the spring of 1932. My musical career and its attendant genius were undoubted. The reputations of Casals, Suggia and Piatigorsky were in jeopardy. More important still, I was deeply in love with a little Belgian redhead named Julie, who played the viola only three short yards to the south-west of me in the Bonn Student Orchestra.

This was by no means a bad band, and on special occasions, such as the Maytime Beethoven festival, a few of us were called upon to augment the excellent City Orchestra when it indulged in its ritual bash at all the Beethoven symphonies, overtures and concertos.

I need hardly say that I was not among those few. Nor, thank heavens, was Julie. Nor Willie Smith. Willie was a huge red-faced Scotsman who chewed tobacco, recited too much Burns and played the bassoon. He had a bristling moustache and a coiffure like a shaving brush. His name ought to have been Hamish McDougall, or some such, but to the disappointment of the Germans it was only Willie Smith.

He was killed at Cleves, serving with the 15th Scottish Division. At the risk of appearing callous, I must say I'm surprised the Germans didn't have a go at Willie long before, because he used to walk up and down the Lessingstrasse every Saturday night playing *Scotland the Brave* and *The 92nd's Farewell to Gibraltar* on the pipes. Bagpipes are an acquired taste, and its acquisition requires a greater sense of humour than had been vouchsafed to the inhabitants of the Lessingstrasse where Willie and I lodged with Professor Dr. Kremer. Willie's only supporter apart from myself was little Hans Mahler, the postmaster's son. Somehow, Hans, Julie and I always managed to get a belligerent Willie up to bed before the protests grew too vehement. Hans lived over his father's post office near the level-crossing and played the French horn in our band. When we reached the star part for the horn in the last movement of Beethoven's *Seventh*, Hans used to clamber to his feet in ecstasy, which is not an easy thing to do while playing the French horn. Willie used to shout, "Well wound, Hans; oh, well wound, sir." Hans was a dear and was the only German in the little gang of us that used to go around together. There was also a quiet and luminous Italian whose real name I've forgotten. He led the second violins and sometimes conducted us at rehearsals. We called him Toscanini and we loved him dearly. Our sixth and last member was another Belgian called Constantin. He played the trumpet and had infamous designs on Julie.

We six went around together, not I think from xenophobia but largely by accident. Our German colleagues certainly treated us with kindness and courtesy. They asked us to their parties and their parents invited us into their homes, but we never felt really comfortable nor, I think, did they.

Bonn in 1932, despite Hitler on the horizon, was still a city of operetta and schmaltz. I think it's a dreadful place now. Brendan Bracken said Bonn looked as if Welwyn Garden City had given birth to a child by Whitehall. A university town and a federal capital just won't mix.

"Was ist hier abends zu tuen?" I asked the barman in the Königshof when I first went back after the war.

"Das grosse nichts," he replied, truthfully but disloyally, and he was right. The old theory about there having once been a nightlife in Bonn but she went to live in Düsseldorf is justified.

But 1932 was different. We sailed up and down the Rhine. Toscanini played the guitar and we all sang the last act of *Figaro* and drank too much Moselwein. We danced under the linden trees by the river, took our sandwiches up the Siebengebirge and went as often as we could to the opera in Cologne.

That was my undoing. One day Hans told us that there was a new production of *Die Meistersinger* brewing; the first night was bound to be an event in Cologne's operatic history and we ought to be there. We must be there, nothing could stop us, and I, as the organising and financial genius of the party, was to get the tickets and arrange the whole outing.

I thundered into action. I collected the right money, I fixed the right officials, and assembled my flock ten minutes before curtain time outside the gallery entrance of the Cologne Opera. At nine minutes before curtain time it became painfully obvious to my flock, and even more so to me, that their organising genius had got tickets for the wrong night. There was nothing that could be done about it, though my friends suggested a lot that could be done about me. When the uproar had finally subsided it was the ever-helpful Hans who came to my rescue. Spilt milk was mentioned and the uselessness of crying over it. Another opportunity would doubtless present itself (it never did) and in the meantime Hans had a brainwave. Hitler was due to speak on the city football ground in thirty minutes time. Had any of us ever heard him speak? We had not. Did we realise the importance of this man, what he would do for his country, the impact he would eventually have on Germany and the world? Not only that, Hitler was the greatest orator of all time. Hear him we must.

Speaking for myself I'm not quite sure what I realised about Hitler in the spring of 1932. I was sufficiently interested in politics to realise that the feeling in Britain about Nazism had far outgrown the initial reactions of ridicule and distrust. But I cannot honestly pretend that in 1932 I took Hitler seriously.

But it was not Hitler the politician, nor Hitler the tyrant to be, that Hans really wanted us to see. It was Hitler the rabble-rouser, Hitler the mob orator, the spellbinder that Hans was determined his foreign friends should hear. With some misgivings we agreed to go.

Even at the age of seventeen I had become fascinated by the art of oratory and the effect that a gifted speaker could have upon his audience. I had heard Lloyd George once or twice, but only when he was past his best. I had heard and been inspired by Churchill, but only in a private gathering. The cold and clinical John Simon had fascinated me, but his was the fascination of the cobra, and Ramsay Macdonald I had unjustly believed to be drunk. Baldwin I thought, and still think, could woo, cosset and win the confidence of an audience more effectively than any man I ever heard. None of these had I witnessed in command of a really big meeting, and Bevan, excelling in the Commons, and Hore Belisha, superb on the platform, were still to come.

Half curious, half reluctant, I trudged along beside my friends in the crowd that was pushing and singing its way to the stadium.

The Nazis had not then brought the mass rally to the stylised perfection it ultimately achieved. But the meeting was successful enough in all conscience. The drums, the trumpets, the flags and lights, the thunder of the captains and the shouting – all made their mark and the mark was almost hypnotically effective. The tension steadily mounted.

Then into the spotlight – with the hysterical cheering and ascending fanfares – strode the Führer himself; Hitler the spellbinder, the magician, Hitler the orator of all time.

Orator, my foot! My disillusionment was complete. I knew enough German to realise that Hitler's was bad. His voice was harsh and uncompelling and his choice of language trite. In a speech of well over an hour he hardly used an expression that could not be found in a student's phrase book. His gestures were rudimentary and his production and the presentation of his personality were those of a ninth-rate Shakespearean ham. The whole effect was absurd.

If this ridiculous and contemptible figure wove no spell for me, my friends and I were in a tiny and unsympathetic minority of six. Fifty thousand Germans were carried away on a steadily mounting wave of hysteria, the ugly wave that was to become all too familiar in the years to come. Obviously they wanted to be carried away and I clearly did not. Perhaps my imperfect German denied to me those nuances and inflection of meaning that might win a grudging respect for an orator's professional skill. All I experienced was bewilderment that such technical incompetence could produce such a staggering result.

I mentioned a minority of six. I'm wrong. A minority of five. Willie, of course, agreed with me and so, I think, did the others. Even Julie, who had not spoken to me since the debacle outside the opera, consented to hold my hand during a tirade about the evildoing of the colonial powers.

But halfway through Hitler's peroration I caught

23

sight of Hans's face. Dear, kind, gentle Hans. He was aglow with adulation. He was a man transported and he remained in a trance long after we had clambered aboard our tram back to Bonn.

He became a fervent Nazi and was eventually sentenced to life imprisonment for war crimes by the French.

Hans disillusioned me more than Hitler. To this day I cannot understand how the Germans, one of the most cultured, industrious and sophisticated peoples in the world, could suddenly, willingly and almost unanimously, have hurled themselves into the greatest uncleanness that history has ever known.

5

Down with August!

I've always had a bee in my bonnet about August and it has not been affected by the fact that they've changed the date of the August Bank Holiday. It used to be the eighth Monday after Trinity, but now it tends to fall on the first Monday before Muckspreading, or thereabouts. This has naturally proved confusing, so most people take both Mondays off just to make sure.

Come to think of it, most people seem to take the whole of August off, anyway. You can't get anything done, although, oddly enough, there are still plenty of people around who are ready to do you. Bills continue to glide through the letter-box, but if you ring up and say that you can't possibly have had 127 trunk calls to Wolverhampton in one week because your phone was out of order, they say they're sorry but the computer's gone on holiday, and will you please complain again in September.

Parking tickets continue to fall as thick as leaves in Vallombrosa, but if you go round to explain that it can't be you they're grumbling about because your car has been in the garage for three months waiting for a spare part, you'll find the office shut, for the hols, and a notice saying, "Try Wandsworth Civic Centre".

Frankly, I don't understand this. When you consider all the awful things that have happened to us in August you'd have thought that we would be on our toes, and ready to take on all comers. Not a bit of it. And the rot didn't set in yesterday, either.

Go back to 55 BC, and what do we find? We find Julius Caesar turning up uninvited on the beach at

Broadstairs right in the middle of the August holidays. This was not only tiresome, but tactless. Although his nephew, Augustus, named the month of August after himself, he had magnanimously named July after Julius. July, therefore, would have been a more fitting month for the outing. But no, August it was, and bless me if Caesar wasn't back again the next August, and with a much stronger cast; five Legions and 2,000 Cavalry, no less. All tourist towns like repeat business, but that must have been a bit much for the back streets of Broadstairs, and everyone was obviously relieved when Caesar pushed off to the north. Unfortunately, he got bogged down at Dagenham, which, as any Ford shareholder could have told him, was only to be expected. At Colchester worse befell. There Caesar lost his 2 i/c., C. Publius Severus, poisoned by a bad oyster. August you see; no "R" in the month.

And so it went on. In August 1667 the Dutch Fleet sailed up the Medway, and scant good came of that. Nobody paying attention, that was the trouble. Just as nobody was paying attention when the Great Train Robbery was pulled off in August 1963, or when Lord Beaverbrook bought *The Daily Express* in the August of 1916.

Sir Francis Drake was the man largely responsible for this couldn't-care-less approach. It was, of course, in August that he put paid to the Spanish Armada, having refused to accelerate his game of bowls for a lot of bumptious dagoes. Actually, this was just a simple piece of West Country one-upmanship on Drake's part, and the silly foreigners fell for it. So far from being caught on the hop, Sir Francis had everything nicely laid on; all kegs properly powdered, all drums at the ready, and the Cap'n very far from sleeping there below. Even in 1588 we were not quite so casual as we seemed.

I don't think, however, that this dawned on the Spaniards, or on any of their successors who have subsequently wished us ill. August, they felt, would automatically catch us napping, and was therefore the right time of the year to try and do us a mischief. And, boy, have they tried!

The Kaiser tried in August 1914. Our grandparents were paddling at Broadstairs, but Winston assures us in his little book that "the Army was ready, the Navy was ready, the Civil Service was ready; all my plans worked perfectly." Even allowing for Churchillian hyperbole, they didn't work so badly at that.

Nor did they in 1939. There were, of course, a few lacunae. Hitler became Chancellor of the German Reich in 1934 (guess when? 2 August) and subsequently entered into his non-aggression Pact with Russia in 1939 (guess when? 23 August). In consequence my regiment was mobilised on 24 August – or almost. What actually happened was that the sub-postmistress who was due to send off our mobilisation papers must have been on holiday herself, and my own marching orders turned up so late that they nearly had to start the War without me. But my C.O. was very nice about it, and said it really didn't matter at all.

We certainly do lay ourselves open for trouble in August. We invite disaster, and are peeved when we get it. We beaver away in secret behind the scenes, and are then hurt if nobody takes us seriously. During World War I Bert Thomas produced a cartoon of a whimsical and battered Tommy lighting his pipe, and under it the caption "'Arf a mo', Kaiser." This sentiment, infuriating to our enemies and to such friends as we still possess, is a source of smug satisfaction to ourselves. It typifies, we like to think, our feeling for expert improvisation, and our refusal, like Sir Francis Drake, to be jockeyed into rearranging our priorities. But I still think it's tempting Providence.

In the Summer of 1944 I was staying with a few friends near a village called Douvres la Deliverande, in Normandy. Unfortunately, it still harboured some Germans whose presence had been overlooked by the 3rd Canadian Division on their way up North. The Germans, in their rather caddish manner, started to take pot-shots at our Brigadier on his way to the Mobile Bath Unit. "Get rid of them," he said, "at once." We planned an operation for the next evening, Thursday, at 9 p.m. We consulted our advisers. Bombardier Bean shook his head, sadly. "Thursday, at 2100 hours?" he said. "No, Sir, sorry, Sir. Not on, Sir. That's ITMA."

ITMA was a radio programme of inspired lunacy. It soon became so popular that nobody could be expected to go into battle whilst it was on the air. The enemy discovered this, and attacked so frequently at 9 p.m. on a Thursday that ITMA had to be broadcast at differing times and dates. This was carrying the doctrines of Sir Francis Drake and Bert Thomas to extremes.

Even after the War we persisted in thinking that just because we were all on holiday in August ourselves, people would leave us alone. The Berlin crisis, the confrontation with Nasser, and the Persian oil row of 1951, all ought to have reminded us how vulnerable we still are in August. Admittedly this August hasn't been so bad as some, but I'm glad it's over and done with, all the same. On the Glorious Twelfth it was reported from the Moors that the grouse seemed a little bit jumpy. A day or two later the same trouble was reported about the Dollar. The weather was, as usual, summery. Our local Bring and Buy Sale was not just washed out – it was sluiced out. But *sluiced*. But then, the weather always is vile in August; September is infinitely better. Charles II maintained that a man could be usefully employed out of doors in England for more days than in any other country in the world, and although I am not sure I would consider Charles II an expert on employment *out* of doors, I think he had a point. But even he thought nothing of August. He said it gave him gout.

Nasser, Hitler, the Kaiser, and now gout. It's just too much. I think that August should be abolished.

6
My Masters

Some while ago, I came across a life of the late Victor Cazalet tucked away in the book-shelves of the House of Lords Library. I started to browse through it. Victor had been a friend of my father's in the Commons but I myself had only known him slightly; I remembered him as a friendly back-bencher but, more notably, as a brilliant squash player. I also remember that I had a drink in his company the night before he died. He was killed in an air crash at Gibraltar in which the distinguished but controversial Polish General Sikorski was also killed and which eventually resulted in much ugly litigation. I happened to be stationed in Gib at the time so I was naturally interested to see what the book had to say about it all.

After a short while, I put it sadly aside. The plain fact was that although Victor Cazalet may have merited a short monograph, he didn't really deserve a whole book. I returned it to the library and ran my eye along the shelves. I was interested and indeed startled to discover how many people, who were the subjects of biographies, and even more of autobiographies, fell into the same category as Victor Cazalet. They were worthy of more than an obituary notice in *The Times* or an entry in the *Dictionary of National Biography* but not of a full-blown book.

And so an idea came into my head for a book of my own. I would make a collection of essays about people whom I had myself known well and who in my opinion deserved much more than that *Times* obituary notice but less than a whole book. I would limit myself to those who were no longer alive because this would minimise the risk of umbrage or worse. I would call the book "My Masters" and would thereby confine it to people whom I had had the pleasure, or otherwise, of once having had to obey. And I would not write about anybody who had already appeared between covers. A book from me on Winston Churchill or Monty or Anthony Eden would hardly seem appropriate, although I had served under them all, even if at some distance.

Where then, should I start? I began to rough out some notes.

One of the first people from whom I had taken orders was obviously Nanny. She had come to my grandparents in Norwich as a tweeny-maid of sixteen and had died there during the war in her nineties. A kindly commanding officer granted me compassionate leave but I only reached Norwich in time for her funeral. Her name was Louisa Howlett and her father had driven the pilot train that ran between Norwich and Cromer. She gave me my first Bible in which is inscribed in her firm, clear hand: "Stormont. Remember 'the fear of the Lord is the beginning of wisdom'." Though I loved her dearly, and shared some of her disapproval of Queen Victoria, I'm afraid my memories of her would hardly stretch to more than a very short essay, but she would certainly be worth it.

My thoughts next turned to the Head Master of my prep school, Highfield at Liphook. Canon W. R. Mills was a pompous, sanctimonious old snob and I was extremely fond of him. He was a born teacher and I owe to him my reverence for the language of the Authorised Version and the Book of Common Prayer. He also realised that my contributions to the Debating Society were more notable than my performance on the cricket field and he gave me appropriate encouragement. He did, however, write in the school magazine that I should remember that it is not necessary to be noisy in order to be convincing.

I was miserably unhappy at Highfield. I don't lay this at the door of Canon Mills who was an understanding and kindly man. I blame it on the barbaric British practice of tearing an eight year old boy away from his home and his parents at the very moment he most needs their support and guidance. I sent my own son to Highfield because I supposed it was the right thing to do, but I don't believe he was much happier than I was.

H. A. Vachell in *The Hill* (his novel about Harrow) seeks to justify our boarding school system by explaining that it makes a man of you. Well, possibly; though I can think of other means that have been tried with greater success.

There was, however, one small but not unrelated incident that I remember from the early days of the war. My battery was stationed in a laundry near Royston. The Orderly Sgt. and I were walking around late one night. We suddenly heard a disturbing noise coming from behind one of the ironing tables. We strolled across and peered down at what proved to be one of our best young men sobbing his heart out. We both knew him well. He was a tough boy who lived with his parents over their butcher's shop in Putney. I looked at the Orderly Sgt. and he shook his head, as sympathetically as any Gunner Sgt. can shake a head. "That's a good boy," he said, "a very good boy. But I think it's probably the first time he's ever slept away from home." Maybe Vachell has something, after all.

I last saw Canon Mills at our wedding. He gave us some window boxes as a wedding present and had taken the trouble to check them for size before doing so.

After he died they launched an appeal for a suitable memorial. I was reaching for my cheque book when I caught sight of his will, published in *The Times*. My dear revered old Headmaster had left over £250,000. I thought of the huge fees my father had paid, I thought of the second helpings we had always been denied, I thought of the cold showers to save fuel bills and I put my cheque book back in my pocket. And then I thought of the Authorised Version and the Book of Common Prayer, and took it out again. Yes, Canon Mills was certainly worth a mention.

In September of 1927 I went on from Highfield to Winchester. I was in "K" House (Beloe's) and my next master was my Housedon, Hal Tyndale. He was one of the most unlikeable men I have ever known. This view is widely shared so it cannot have been entirely my fault. To this day, however, I don't know exactly what it was that still gives all his old pupils the creeps whenever they have cause to remember him.

On the credit side, there was much to commend him. He was an old Wykehamist himself and full of sound Wykehamical lore. He had been a fine mountaineer until a savage war wound in his foot put an end to his sport. He was a liberal-minded man and a first class teacher. Perhaps his nick-name "The Greaser" may contain a clue to his unpopularity. I personally think particularly ill of him because he allowed his House to acquire a savage and well-remembered reputation for bullying. Either he knew what was going on and shut his eyes to it or he didn't know what was going on, which he certainly ought to have done, and which I'm inclined to regard as even more reprehensible.

Being the only Jew in the school was of little help to me and it was not until I was about seventeen and big enough to knock other people about that I began to enjoy Winchester.

At the time of which I am writing, the fagging system was widespread at most British Public Schools though I believe it is now on the way out. At Winchester, small boys were assigned to large boys and charged with the duties of pressing their trousers and polishing their Sam Browne belts for OTC parades. These small boys went by the odd name of clothes-cads and the prefect for whom I slaved was one Nicholas Monsarrat, later to become the distinguished author of *The Cruel Sea* and other fierce works. He himself, I am glad to say, was not fierce at all. He was a vague, scholarly but kind taskmaster.

32

Fortunately, I served other masters at Winchester who were more attractive than Hal Tyndale. Such a one was Sir George Dyson, our music don. (Masters at Winchester were always called dons just as we boys, however small, were always referred to as men.) We were a very musical school in my day and this was largely to the credit of George Dyson, who was a most outstanding musician. He looked like a plumber's mate but could inspire a gangling mob of teenagers in the Glee Club to sing like the morning stars. He played the organ in chapel and trained the choir which, although I sang in it myself for three years, was not a bad nest of singing birds.

He conducted and trained the school orchestra. I played the 'cello which I learned off Miss Alcock whose father was the organist in Salisbury Cathedral. My co-cellist on the first desk was a burly red-head named Robert Irving. His own father was a House don in the school and brother-in-law to his fellow Alpinist, Hal Tyndale. Robert himself never climbed after his sister died in a dreadful mountaineering accident. Robert was a first-class classical scholar (and Winchester has and always has had exacting standards), a stalwart footballer, an excellent pianist and cellist but (in my opinion though not his) only a second class tenor. He took a brilliant scholarship to New College, joined the RAF where he was much decorated for gallantry, bought some questionable racehorses and retired to New York where, for twenty-five years, he has conducted the City's ballet orchestra with immense distinction. He comes home every year for Ascot and is a welcome guest conductor at Covent Garden. What Horace Walpole would have called a round man. When I couldn't manage the more difficult 'cello passages, I would raise my bow a millimetre from the strings and glance at Robert who would then scrape away doubly hard. I knew that he knew but he never let on. A lovely as well as a round man.

Our violas were led by Humphrey Searle who subsequently became a distinguished but to me, unintelligible composer. George Dyson was himself also a composer of distinction but easier to understand than Searle. His best work is his *Canterbury Pilgrims*, a huge piece now sadly neglected. It was scored for a big orchestra, full choir and four soloists. I was amongst the rank and file at its first performance in Winchester Guildhall. The main body of the troops came from the City Choral and Orchestral Society augmented by the Winchester College choir and orchestra together with a trumpet or two from the Rifle Brigade Depot up on the hill. One of the first violins was a talented and managerial lady named Mrs. Aldridge Lloyd. She had a leggy little blonde daughter who sat in the front row at rehearsals and is now my wife.

George Dyson also taught us harmony and composition. I once announced that one of my chief musical ambitions was to rescore Brahms's double concerto for violin and 'cello as a single concerto for 'cello. He said that was fine but before I tried my hand at it I'd better learn to score an ordinary four part hymn that wasn't as full of consecutive fifths as mine always seemed to be.

He was also, oddly enough, a great expert on bombs and grenades and one of his favourite parlour tricks was to dismantle a 36 Mills bomb with his eyes blindfold. I do not believe, however, that there were many parlours in which this particular trick was actually brought off nor, I suppose, was it in great demand at the Royal College of Music whose Principal he eventually became. Apart from this, I remember him as an inspiring if unconventional master.

Winchester's Headmaster also comes within my terms of reference. He was the Rev. Alwyn Terrell Petre Williams. He had come up from the office of Second Master and left us to become, in turn, Dean of Christ Church, Bishop of Durham and ultimately Bishop of Winchester. His nick-name was History Bill but this was only mentioned under bated breath because we all regarded him as first cousin to God which is not the way most Headmasters are regarded today.

I only met the Headmaster personally on one occasion and it was not a happy one. In 1931 a General Election was called and in the middle of term at that. I was already keenly interested in politics and asked if I could accept an invitation, which I had received, to address the electorate in the marshalling yards of Eastleigh railway station. Permission was curtly refused.

However, a mock election meeting was staged in Sir Christopher Wren's splendid school hall. I was one of six selected to address the multitude. I made what I considered to be a calm and statesmanlike oration but unfortunately it ended in uproar. The meeting then adjourned, but the uproar continued until the audience reached Morgan's bicycle shop in Kingsgate Street where it developed into an affray.

Next morning, I was sent for by the Headman and charged with responsibility for this embarrassing turn of events. The politician, budding within me, came to the fore and I talked my way out of it but on leaving the Presence, the Headman gave me what could undoubtedly be classified as A LOOK.

I left Winchester before my time in order to go out to South Africa on one of the Schoolboys' Empire Tours which were very popular in those days. Two boys were selected from each of about twenty Public Schools and the vacancies were in great demand. We journeyed by rail from the Cape to the Victoria Falls and back. The master in charge was a splendid Green Jacket Brigadier named Hugo Watson. He was also an old Wykehamist and he saw to it that I never once stayed in a hotel in the whole five months we were away. I was invariably invited to stay with some friendly old Wykehamist. I went out a nervous schoolboy and came back almost grown-up.

From there I went to study German and music at Bonn University about which I have already written in Chapter 4. I think I might have learnt a little more of the 'cello if my master (a diminutive Basque) had not been so fond of garlic as to make close attention uncomfortable. I could not pronounce let alone spell his name but he would earn a mention in my book if only for his farewell kiss when I left the University.

In the autumn of 1932 I went up to Oxford and spent at Christ Church three of the most enjoyable years of my life. There were many there who, whether they liked it or not, could have properly been included amongst my masters and within my terms of reference.

First, of course, came the Dean. Dean White was a dear little gnome of a man with a beautiful handwriting but, alas, more than fine caligraphy is needed for the dual and almost impossible task of running a busy cathedral and a truculent college. Dr. White could be remembered as one of our most charming but not one of our greatest incumbents.

He was succeeded in office by none other than History Bill from Winchester who was (thanks to his close relationship with the Almighty) made of sterner stuff. Dean White was alleged to have known none of his undergraduates either by name or by sight. Dean Williams certainly knew one of them and that unfortunately was me.

In 1934 I was serving as Secretary of the University Conservative Association. Another General Election was called and the City's Member of Parliament, Captain Bourne, the distinguished oarsman, decided that as he was also Deputy Speaker of the Commons he ought not to take too controversial a part in the forthcoming campaign. Would we undergraduate Tories care to lend a hand? You bet we would!

I met the Dean one afternoon crossing Tom Quad. He beckoned me over. He presumed, he said, that I should be unable to keep quiet during the following weeks but he hoped there would be no repetition of that regrettable fracas outside Morgan's bicycle shop in Kingsgate Street some years ago. His hope was unfulfilled and the conclusion of our first political meeting would have made l'affaire Morgan look very small beer.

36

Fortunately, the Dean was away from Oxford and we were able to persuade Bobbie Longden, the Junior Censor (who knew not Kingsgate Street, Winchester) that it was all the fault of those beastly Bolshies. Bobbie was a charming, handsome man. He left Oxford to become Headmaster of Wellington and was killed during the blitz whilst shepherding his flock into an air raid shelter. Sadly, therefore, he would have fallen within my terms of reference.

My tutor, S. N. Grant Bailey, does not fill my bill for he is happily still alive though I have lost all track of him. His knowledge of the law was great, greater, unfortunately, than his ability to impart it. At the approach of the Law Finals most of his pupils were to be found with Mr. Cousins, the law crammer, who lived in the High in term time and ran splendid reading parties from his home at Lamorna Cove in the summer.

It was and still is said of Oxford dons that too few of them have ever been taught how to teach. I can remember at least two exceptions who would both be candidates for my book. One was the redoubtable Sonners of Brasenose (William Teulon Sonnenschein Stallybrass). He taught us criminal law. One day at the end of a meaty lecture on justifiable homicide he called me up to him. "I have reason to believe," he said abruptly, "that your mother was a Miss Phoebe Chune Fletcher. I think you should know that I once wished to marry her." The feather had not then been plucked with which you could have knocked me down and I rushed off to telephone my mother. She was fussy about this sort of thing and she made me reassure her, therefore, that it was from Sonners himself that I had received this startling information. Then she just said, "Yes, that is so and, now, what is the rest of your news?'

I also sat at the feet of Arthur Goodhart, one of the greatest legal pundits of his day. Shortly before he died I was asked to take part in a TV series in which you could select and discuss somebody whom you felt had much influenced your life. Even though he had once prevented me from wearing hunting clothes whilst sitting for an early morning exam in jurisprudence, I had held Arthur Goodhart in warm affection even since I left Oxford. So I chose him as my subject and he did not seem displeased with my efforts. He was a great master and a very sweet man – almost worth a whole book in addition to his own distinguished work in the Law Quarterly Review and elsewhere.

To return to Dean Williams. He went on up to Durham as Bishop which quietly pleased us Wykehamists because the Headmaster of Eton, the rather forward Dr. Cyril Alington, had only gone to Durham as Dean. History Bill came back to Winchester as Bishop which is not the usual pattern of preferment. He spoke seldom in the House of Lords and not, I'm afraid, very effectively. I ran into him once outside my Club, the Carlton, in St. James's Street. His head was swathed in bandages. He had apparently been inspecting repairs to one of his churches when a load of builders' hardware had descended suddenly upon him from on high, breaking his nose and generally shaking him up badly. I duly commiserated with him and reminded him that there was respectable precedent for such a mishap. A pot of paint had once descended from Michelangelo's eyrie in the Sistine Chapel and narrowly missed the Pope haranguing him from below. "That was not an accident," said the Bishop; "it was deliberate and I trust you are making no such suggestions concerning my own encounter." This was about the nearest I ever knew the Bishop get to a joke.

Mulling over my list of Oxford masters, I suddenly noticed a serious omission. Sgt. Percy Rimes of the 16/5 Lancers, our instructor in horsemastership in the OTC was also a remarkable man. Not only was he a first class teacher but he managed to steer successfully the difficult course between over-familiarity with his unruly undergradutate troops and unacceptably strict discipline. He could swear at you without repeating himself for many minutes and without once using a dirty word. This is quite an art.

Many years later I found that by odd coincidence my step-daughter Venetia was being taught to ride by Percy at her boarding school near Buntingford. I'm proud to say that she proved a much apter pupil than I, as those will bear witness who have followed her riding a dashing side-saddle with the Quorn.

I have not been able to find if Sgt. Rimes is still alive or is even now discussing martingales and surcingles with the Valkyrie in Valhalla. In either case, I offer a respectful salute to his horsemastership.

I had joined the OTC not only to learn the military arts but, more important, to be able to hunt and play polo. I bought a flea-bitten old mare from the Scots Greys for £50. She was named Nightdress because she was white and pulled up easily. She was no more suited to polo than I, but I hunted her regularly with the South Oxfordshire hounds and even risked my neck in the occasional point-to-point. I was never once placed but, equally, I never once failed to finish the course. Well, you can't have everything.

After leaving Oxford I started to read for the Bar. My tutors were the celebrated crammers, Gibson & Weldon, in Chancery Lane who, if only for the confidences they hold, are worth a whole book to themselves. I also spent some months with Messrs. Whinney, Smith and Whinney, the distinguished chartered accountants in Old Jewry. My father thought, and I now share that view, that a knowledge of accountancy is the key that opens all the best doors in the world of commerce. This view was doubtless shared by Sir Charles Palmour, the senior partner, but he did not think the key was likely to be found in my particular pocket and said so politely but firmly.

I later spent several months in preparation for the Bar with Farrer & Co. of Lincolns Inn Fields, solicitors to the Queen and a firm which took long to acknowledge the invention of the typewriter. Technically, my masters were Cecil Webb and Sir Leslie Farrer. Leslie, had it not been for an impediment in his speech, would have obviously gone to the Bar and thence to the Court of Appeal. In practice, however, my real masters were the clerks who showed me every rat-hole in the Law Courts, taught me every judge's nick-name and the way to the heart of every barmaid in Carey Street. But the time soon came when I must find someone who would accept me as a pupil in chambers. Grant-Bailey of Christ Church found such a one for me. Francis Skone James of 5 New Square became my master in the law and I was mighty lucky to find him willing to take me. He was a delightful man of senatorial mien. He possessed an immense knowledge of the law but less of practical matters such as blown fuses, parking regulations, timetables and so on. His speciality was Copyright (in which esoteric branch of the law his son has followed him). He was looking for someone who could read a musical score. I persuaded Skone James that Beethoven and Bach were mere beginners compared with myself and I got the job.

I had spent six happy months under his pupil-mastership when the war broke out. He bade me farewell, and advised me not to be taken prisoner-of-war as he had been. I did not see him again for six and a half years when I walked back into chambers after my de-mob. He looked up and said simply, "What kept you?" He renewed my pupilship as if little had happened and the chambers eventually invited me to stay on permanently which is a nice thing to happen to any young barrister. I was able to help him with the proof-reading of his edition of Copinger on Copyright and I dined as his guest when he was appointed Treasurer of the Middle Temple. Straight into my book.

Now what about those six and a half years? How many masters? How many fall within my parameters? For nearly a year, for instance, whilst serving in the Military Operations Directorate at the War Office, our particular branch answered regularly to Field Marshal Lord Alanbroke about whom much, perhaps too much, has already been written, some of it by himself. Few people come out of an autobiography with as high a reputation as when they went in, but I will content myself by saying that he was one of the finest men I have ever met. My immediate boss was known as Simbo but he, as General Sir Frank Simpson, is happily still alive and a good example of the reason why amateur soldiers like myself get angry when we have to listen to criticism of the regular officer. I never cease to be astonished at the high standards attained by the regular soldier in wartime in the face of all the obstructions, both political and financial, which are put in his way in times of peace.

Like any other soldier I must have served hundreds of masters during the war, most of whom would now fall within my terms of reference. I would single out one only for inclusion and for two sound reasons. Few outside his immediate circle will have heard his name and he was a most unusual and outstanding man.

That name was Reggie Parminter and I served as his Brigade Major in Normandy. He started and ended the war as a Brigadier in which respect he must have been almost unique. Apparently he had a row with his Corps Commander on some exercise and although the Corps Commander was soon seen through by Higher Authority and duly sacked, the black mark against Reggie's name must always have counted. So, possibly, did his appearance and demeanour. Although he wore two DSO's and two MC's, he also wore a monocle and a nonchalance to match. He was almost circular in shape, blankly refused to wear battle dress or a tin hat, had been Commandant of the Kneller Hall School of Music, Mayor of Gibraltar and spoke fluent French. He never raised his voice and I never once knew him to show the slightest signs of fear or anger. Nor did he ever issue a written order as far as I can remember. He simply told us what he had in mind and expected us to get on with it, and such was the affection and respect in which we all held him that get on with it we did. Not all of these characteristics could have commended him to the Military Secretary's Office.

I went to see him frequently in Millbank Military Hospital during his last long and dreadful illness. His only complaint was that the doctors limited him to two whiskys a day; the first time, he said, that the RAMC had ever let him down. He deserved a better leave-taking and much better treatment by his superior officers.

Back to 5 New Square. Once I had completed my pupilage I had, technically, no master but was like any other fledgling barrister starving cheerfully on my own. In point of fact, my real master was my clerk, Tivey, who bullied, cajoled, hustled and bustled me about until I started to build up something which might have been light-heartedly referred to as a practice.

Then in 1952 I was invited to join HMG as a very junior Minister and since a political life had always been my real ambition, I put my wig into its black tin box, offered grateful thanks to Skone James and headed for Whitehall.

I'm not sure if one's Chief Whip would technically count as a master but the Earl Fortescue MC certainly behaved as one. Tim Fortescue had not commanded the Royal Scots Greys for nothing, and although he never pretended to know much about politics you knew well enough that if he wanted you to do this or say that or be somewhere at a certain time, you were going to do, say and be there or else.

As Under Secretary of State at the Home Office, I had two masters both of whom fill my bill. One was Gwilym Lloyd-George the Home Secretary and the other, Sir Frank Newsam, the Permanent Head of the Office. Both deserve to be remembered.

Gwil was a delightful man – an experienced old political hand; cheerful, loyal, wily and bone-idle. Whenever he was faced with a sticky problem (and the Home Office is the repository of all the stickiest problems) he would change the subject and tell you some amusing new story about his father.

Power, therefore, rested with the moody and difficult Frank Newsam and he certainly knew how to use it. Some times he went too far and misused it because most of his staff, and I even more so, were scared stiff of him, so that when he made a mistake (which he very seldom did) there were few who had the courage to say so.

One such mistake was the Government's decision to ban heroin. The story is all in Hansard so I need not set it out again. Suffice it to say that not only did the Home Office misjudge the views of the medical profession on the clinical value of this admittedly dangerous drug, they misjudged even more seriously their own legal power to ban it. So humble pie had to be eaten and it was I who had to present that pie to the House of Lords.

What follows is not in Hansard. Sir Frank Newsam sent for me just before I set off. "We have made a serious blunder," he said, "and you will have to admit it. You will also have the worst quarter of an hour of your political life. You will have to take all the blame yourself and will in no way implicate any particular department or official. I will deal with that in due course. Please come in when you get back and tell me how it went. Is that clear?"

I counted ten and screwed up my courage to the sticking point. "Sir Frank," I said, "I do actually know the basic rules of ministerial etiquette but I don't think I'm coming back to tell you how it went. Wouldn't you like to come across to the House to see for yourself how I get on?"

He glared at me and I thought, Good Lord, what have I said? Then he got up very slowly, took his bowler hat off its stand, pushed me through the door and then further, in silence, across Parliament Square. He sat in the official box throughout the whole of that horrible debate.

Just as I got up to speak, Gwil Lloyd-George slipped unexpectedly into the House and took his seat on the steps of the throne where Privy Councillors from the

Commons are entitled to sit. When it was all over, he sent his battered lieutenant a heartening little note: "You couldn't have done better."

Frank Newsam also sent me a note. It was differently worded. "It might have been worse!" *Autres maîtres, autres moeurs.*

In 1957, I was moved on to the Ministry of Defence where many who were my masters are still alive and accordingly out of reach. The unshiftable Duncan Sandys was the Minister and Sir Richard Powell our Permanent Secretary. Marshal of the RAF, Dickie Dixson, was the Chief of the Defence Staff; Lord Mountbatten, Air Chief Marshal Sir Dermot Boyle and General Sir Gerald Templer were the Chiefs of their respective Staffs. Their ranks and titles have, of course, since changed but one thing they all had in common which, I suspect, may have taken some while to change. At no time that I can remember were all of them on speaking terms with Duncan or with each other. If my memory is at fault and they occasionally were, it was not due to me, hard though I tried. It must have been due to the calm and elegant Freda Smith who worked in the private office and was the possessor of the most unturned hair and the most unbattable eyelid in Whitehall.

On the day upon which our only son Benjamin was born, my two splendid secretaries, Miss Powell and Mr. Harry Godfrey, marked the occasion by taking the red tape off a legal brief I was to read upon my arrival in the office and substituting a huge blue ribbon. I think that was my happiest memory of the Ministry of Defence.

My bank manager and my trustees (realistic masters) reacted differently. They said that I must now face facts, ask for my cards and start to earn a living.

I reported this to Harold Macmillan, then Prime Minister, at the Blackpool Conservative Conference. He simply said, "What a pity," offered me a glass of champagne and that was that.

A week or two later, Sir Isaac Wolfson invited me to join the board of the Great Universal Stores as a full-time director. I stayed with that remarkable and still vigorous entrepreneur for eight years, being chiefly engaged as Chairman of the organisation's travel division, Global Tours. In 1966, the Chairman of the Cunard Line, Sir Basil Smallpeice, invited me to leave Global and join Cunard as his deputy. He, too, is happily still alive and accordingly ultra vires, though I have a bit more to say about Cunard elsewhere.

Cunard was taken over in 1971 by Trafalgar House with whom I could see no prospect of happy relations. They shared my view, so I packed my bags and they remained packed until the Home Secretary, Reggie Maudling, of affectionate memory invited me to become Chairman of the Tote Board. I have also a bit more to say elsewhere about the Tote and Reggie Maudling as a master who wished to have as little to do with his employee's activities as possible.

From time to time I reviewed this list of masters to make certain that they all properly fulfilled the conditions which I had set myself.

One evening I walked into the House of Lords Bar and ran into Selwyn Lloyd. I had known him well for many years and was one of the few who were privileged to call him by the nick-name Peter, from his college, Peterhouse, at Cambridge. I was fond of him; I was indignant at the slings and arrows to which he had been submitted throughout a long and honourable career of public service but I had never really been able to make him out. He was a cat who walked by himself.

"Have a drink," he said cheerfully. "I'm celebrating."

"Thank you," I said, and, turning to Anne, our splendid barmaid, I asked for a small gin and tonic. (When we are in doubt about something in the Lords, we don't look it up in Erskine May or Who's Who. We look it up in Anne.)

As Anne was reaching for the bottle, I asked Peter what he was celebrating. "Well," he said, "I've at last finished my book on Suez and it's in the hands of the printer. So I can now get down to my next."

"And what's that going to be about?" I asked.

He took a sip at his own drink. "It's going to be a collection of essays about people for whom I've worked and would like to write about but are not worth a whole book each. I'm going to call it *My Masters*."

I caught Anne's eye. "Anne," I said, "make that a large double, will you please."

7
A Garden is a loathsome thing – God wot . . .

The other Sunday we opened our garden to the public in aid of the Red Cross. Whilst that may seem quite a simple sentiment, it embraces, let me assure you, a very complicated operation. Last year, of course, the operation was much simpler because it rained like billy-oh all day and the only member of the public who came near us was Mr. Wilkinson from next door to say that our drains were overflowing into his chicken-run and the girls didn't seem to like it a bit.

This year was different. The sun shone prettily and quite a few people came to see us, including, to do him justice, Mr. Wilkinson.

What exactly they came to see and why they came is a matter of conjecture because our garden, proud though we are of it, is not really of any great moment. No Capability Brown stuff, I'm afraid. No Palladian arches, no gazebos, mazes or sweeping greenswards and, apart from Mr. Wilkinson's particular problem, no lakes. Our garden is a mere 71 × 22 yards (not counting the potting shed) and I paced this out carefully last week knowing that the question was bound to be asked.

Nor could the public have come to admire the splendid elm trees which until last winter had provided us with a windbreak and an elegant northern back-cloth. Alas, they have all fallen victim of the dreaded Dutch Elm Disease which is ravaging our part of Gloucestershire. Incidentally, I think that in order to avoid misunderstanding we had better refer to it in future by its correct botanical name of *Ceratostomella ulmi*. I only mention this because we had the Dutch Ambassador with us for the Cheltenham Gold Cup and the matter arose during dinner on the first night. After listening to our wailings for a few minutes he began to tap quietly on the table with his spoon. "May I speak, please?" he asked. "It is not Dutch Elm Disease. It is English Elm Disease brought here from North America and then correctly identified by a Dutch arboriculturist in the year 1921. There is no cure for it. And now will somebody please pass me the mint sauce?"

There is also another point of definition to be cleared up. When I say that "we" opened the garden I should explain that "we" consists primarily of our head gardener. She has green fingers and the tiresome habit of suggesting that I should do some mowing or shift the compost heap a couple of yards to the North East. I tell her firmly that I am not the gardener's boy. I am, rather, a horticultural technical consultant and my role in the garden is the same as that laid down by Queen Victoria for a Constitutional Monarch – to encourage, to be consulted and to warn. This function can best be exercised from a deck chair on the four days in the year when deck chair operations are in order and by a clear voice through the sitting room window for the rest of the season.

But when you have visitors (even though most of them are only friends and neighbours whose own gardens you yourself will visit when they are opened to the public for the Red Cross next Sunday), conscience dictates a closer involvement. First you have to learn some gardening jargon – not all of it, of course, but just enough to retain your audience until the head gardener comes up with amendments.

I learnt this trick when I first entered the House of Lords some 40 years ago. I was, then as now, a townee but my colleagues were mostly countrymen. Over the tea cups they used to talk about zero-grazing and the normal flight range of the Colorado beetle. I had to sit silent and at a loss for words until the late Lord Halifax one day came to my aid. Learn one sentence by heart, he told me, and then practise slipping it in under your opponent's guard. Don't push it, just slip it in. So, when Noble Lords used to move into their stride on the subject of the late S23 and new Semper Weide types of perennial rye-grass or changes in the modified sheet mulching of young blackcurrent bushes, I would turn a pensive gaze on the portrait of the Fourth Earl of Chesterfield over the cash desk and observe (almost as if talking to myself), "Well, yes, indeed, but times do change don't they? Who would ever have thought that a Friesian would one day turn into a dual purpose animal and with a 0.5 per cent butter-fat increase at that?" My neighbours would nod their heads in agreement and exchange appreciative glances. I have seldom known the trick to fail.

So it is in the garden. If Sunday visitors start asking whether my large-flowered narcissi stems have increased in correct proportion to their flowers or whether it is really true that Mount Hood daffodil leaves are poisonous to cattle, I call in aid Lord Halifax. "Well, perhaps," I say, "but whilst the matter's on my mind, let me remind you that if you're ever troubled with bullfinches in your fruit bushes, hang mothballs in the lower branches and put an old Russian astrakhan hat up at the top. The birds'll think it's a cat." My visitors, to whom this information is probably as novel as it is irrelevant, gaze at me in wide-eyed admiration.

Last year, however, the weather nearly beat us in advance. We wanted to make a real show of the garden so we put in about eight million bulbs. (Well, all right, seven million.) To hit the jackpot, I had said to my head gardener, let's have a few of those Acclamation narcissi I saw at the RHS Show. Very good looking, I thought. "Are you out of your tiny mind?" she replied. "Do you realise that Acclamation costs nearly £10?"

"Is that per 100 or 1,000?"

"Neither, you chump," said my head gardener. "£10 per bulb."

So we did without Acclamation this year and perhaps this was just as well because although Red Cross Day itself was fine, the previous spring weather had been so filthy that only 17 daffs were still standing. They didn't stand much longer and I'll now tell you why.

I am beginning to think there's something about gardens that brings out the worst in everybody. People who are normally quite honest become crooks without compunction. I have even known a Rural Dean take a surreptitious cutting behind his hostess's back. This year, for instance, we advertised T(ND), which means teas, no dogs. Next year I shan't have T or D either. D ruin the lawn and bully our cat, and T involves so much running about with buns and small change that you can't keep an eye on your visitors and see what they're up to. In any case, some people simply do not have the object of the exercise properly in mind. Take Colonel Potterton, for instance. "A cup of tea, Colonel?" I asked. "Well, frankly, no," he replied. "I'd prefer a large whisky and water and no ice."

This was not what we had originally planned but, of course, I went indoors to get it because I'm fond of old Potty even though he does from time to time let the canaries out of our aviary. He doesn't do it on purpose, I need hardly say, but at nesting time (and that means now) he likes to step inside the cage and "see how the little people are getting on." Unfortunately, he invariably leaves the door of the cage open. The canaries know this by now and when he rolls into sight you can hear them saying to each other, "Here he comes, chaps. Anyone for Lechlade or Cirencester? Form up on the right, then."

Well, when I came out with the Colonel's drink, you won't believe what had happened. No, most of the birds were still in situ but nearly all the remaining 17 daffs had been snitched and during the short period I had been absent from the seat of custom, somebody had even gone so far as to leave a dirty, crumpled 50-lire note in our cashbox. There's respectability for you. And on the

Sabbath, too.

The poetess Dorothy Gurney once said something about being nearer God's heart in a garden than anywhere else on earth. Not on a Red Cross Sunday in Gloucestershire, you aren't.

8
Bees under Starters Orders

It was a long time since I had last served in the Home Office, and I cast a nostalgic eye around the Secretary of State's vast room. A beaming Reggie Maudling came forward to greet me.

"Have a drink," he said, coming to the point at once. "I've got a job for you. You've left Cunard, haven't you, so I want you to take on the Chairmanship of the Tote. I'm sure you'll enjoy it. You've always been interested in horses, and your office has a wonderful view of St. Paul's. Oh, and by the way, I'm told that the Tote is bankrupt. Did you say water, or soda?"

"Reggie," I said, "how can a Tote possibly go bankrupt? You take the money in from the punters; you set a little aside for such essential overheads as the Chairman's salary; you then pay out what's left to the lucky winners. How does bankruptcy come into it?"

"Don't stand there asking tomfool questions," said the Home Secretary, "that's exactly what we want you to find out. Get a move on. This is a real challenge."

I'm always suspicious when anything is described as a "real challenge". Crossing Piccadilly is a challenge, drinking carafe plonk in a strange restaurant is a challenge, even staying married is a challenge. I pondered on all this as I wound my way back through the Home Office catacombs. Obviously, holding such an unusual tiger as this by the tail *was* going to be a challenge.

Of course I soon found out why the Tote was in the red. The British Tote is the only one in the world that has to operate in direct competition with 15,000 licensed betting-shops. Very few countries tolerate bookies at all, let alone allow them to operate betting shops. Some countries, Australia and New Zealand for instance, allow bookmakers on the race-course. It is argued, fairly enough, that bookies shouting the odds on the rails adds to the drama and excitement of racing. Punters like to know what odds the market is offering and they enjoy pitting their wits against the book. And the Tote is always there for the quieter customers. But off-course bookmakers are strictly forbidden – except in Britain.

In Britain, only 5 per cent of the bookie's turnover comes from the race-course. The rest comes from the betting-shop and the telephone. Few of the bigger bookies would bother to appear on the race-course if it weren't for the advertisement they gain. The Tote, however, has to operate at every course.

The betting-shop was legalised by H.M.G. in order to do away with the evil of the street-corner bookie, the factory runner, and the corruptible young policeman. I made speeches on the subject when the Bill was going through Parliament, expressing the view that the cash that ought to be finding its way into prize money and the improvement of racing, would now be deflected into the pockets of the bookies. And, for good measure, I pointed out that the Chief Constables had recently expressed the opinion that the bookmaker was at the back of far too much criminal activity for racing's peace of mind. If I'd realised then the damage that the institution of the betting-shop would also do to the Tote, I would probably have mentioned that, too.

Had I also realised that I'd end up one day as Chairman of the Tote, I would probably have expressed all these views in a slightly lower key.

The fact remains, however, that the British punter clearly wants both systems of gambling – Tote and bookie working side by side. Equally clearly, the Government intends him to have them. Tote and bookie have therefore got to get along together. And, although the betting-shop will probably be nationalised one day, it certainly won't be in my day.

Understandably, my appointment received no more than two cheers from the bookmakers' Lobby. Next to the kiddies' Lobby, the doggies' Lobby, the bookies' Lobby is the most efficient I have ever encountered in forty years of political life. The way in which the bookies rearranged the Tote Bill of 1972 was a model of what legitimate lobbying should be. So in the end the Bill wasn't quite what the Government had intended, or the Tote required.

Since moving into my Chair with the wonderful view of St. Paul's I had naturally given a good deal more thought to horse-race betting, in particular, and to the activities of the gambling bug in general.

It has always been held that the Chinese are the world's greatest gamblers, but I think we British may be overtaking them. This is difficult to prove, because the statistics of gambling are notoriously perverse. The fiver that you take to the race-course may turn over half-a-dozen times before it finally comes to rest in Honest Abe's satchel – or, better still, the Tote's cash-box. But all the indications are that we are leading the Chinese by a short head.

The French are more intense in their gambling than we are. The air of concentration that hangs over the French pavement café when the weekly tiercé is under discussion is greater even than that of the Bingo Hall in Bournemouth. In addition to Bingo, the bookies and the Tote, we have, of course, the pools, as well as a proliferation of casinos, not all of which are smiled upon by the Gaming Board. There is, in fact, too much competition for a French-type tiercé ever to find favour here.

The Americans are headstrong gamblers, and I have seen bill-folds flashed at Hialeah and Belmont that would make our Betting Levy look like pin-money. As for Mr. Howard Samuel's Tote operation in New York, it turned me green with envy. But, sophisticated though it is, it does not service the punter all that much more quickly and efficiently than our own rather Heath Robinson arrangement here.

The Spaniards are emotional gamblers, and knives are drawn upon less provocation than would be acceptable, say, in the Working Men's Club at Cleckheaton.

The Japs not only ban bookies from their race-courses, but women, too.

The Dutch have never recovered from the teachings of their sixteenth-century countryman Erasmus. In his view, gambling was worse than sodomy, but he never explained quite why.

The Jamaicans are rash gamblers and will bet upon two flies crawling up the wall. Considering the difficulty of getting one, let alone two flies under starter's orders, this appears very rash indeed. Bees, of course, will obey nobody's orders save those of their Queen and, being workers, are too realistic to gamble.

But the British, in comparison, are now almost compulsive gamblers, and this brings problems in its wake. We spend about two-thousand-millions a year on gambling. This is more than we spend on education – and critics of our current student scene may think that this is as it should be. The Government are in a difficult position. The tax on gambling brings in a tidy sum, but the enormous individual fortunes to be won on the football-pools also bring untidy social problems in their wake. So do "Spot-the-ball" contests, so do the shadier casinos, and so do the profits of some of the bigger bookies.

The Churches take a moderate view. Gambling in excess can be a drug. A whisky-and-soda as a night-cap is all very well, but a bottle a day will kill you. So it is with nicotine, aspirin, and even the seemingly harmless Bingo. A modest flutter on the Derby, say the Churches, is acceptable; but it can very easily become immodest. People are obviously going to gamble, anyhow. The Churches – R.C. and C. of E., at least – accept this, and their proposals are designed to keep gambling within reasonable bounds.

The Tote has its problems, too. The new Law now enables it to operate both as a Tote and as a bookmaker at Starting Price odds. Such an operation does not commend itself to the bookies and the competition is intense.

"I hope you're not going to flaunt yourself now that you're the Government's Turf Accountant," one of the Bishops said to me after the Tote Bill had become Law. I explained to him that we were still on an economic knife-edge, and that it only required a run of bad weather, or bad fields, or bad luck, to push us back into the red. Our competitors, the regular bookies in their betting-shops, wielded a formidable power and expertise. As for flaunting ourselves, though – well, we could hardly meet Reggie Maudling's challenge by sitting back and hoping that business would drift our way. Confucius he say man waste much time standing with mouth wide open waiting for roast duck to fly in.

The view of St. Paul's was certainly splendid, but there was another challenge Reggie Maudling never mentioned at all. The G.P.O. got our address wrong in the 'phone book.

· 9

Churchilliana

Once upon a time there was a monumental row in the correspondence columns of *The Times* about whether or not Winston Churchill was a cruel man. On the whole I think that the uncruels won, led with filial ferocity by his daughter, Mary Soames.

In the unlikely event of my having been asked to join in the argument (for my personal knowledge of Winston was only enough to justify a few sparse notes such as these) I would have said that he wasn't cruel but that he could occasionally be unkind. I say this because he was once unkind to my father and that unkindness I have naturally remembered. So, I think, did my father.

It came about this way. From 1927-1929 my father was Financial Secretary to the Treasury. Winston, as Chancellor of the Exchequer, was his boss. I remember once, on a leave-out day from Winchester, being led in to meet the great man in that magnificent room in the old Treasury overlooking Horse Guards Parade which in those days was the Chancellor's office. He gave me a cigar and a short lecture on the merits of William Kent as an architect. I still treasure both.

During the Committee Stage of the Finance Bill of 1928 Winston, who knew little about finance, as usual left all the donkey work to my father who knew a lot. One evening, there was some minor wrangle about a sixpenny duty on petrol lighters. Father was standing firm when the Colonial Secretary, Leo Amery, slid along the front bench and said that it didn't really seem a matter of life and death and we therefore might as well give way. Seeing that Amery was a Cabinet Minister and my father was not, he duly gave way. Unfortunately, it soon became obvious that it was indeed a matter of life and death because the concession would cut right across the Government's protectionist policies. All hell broke loose, and when peace was restored Winston gave my father the devil of a dressing down and they didn't speak for quite a while. Winston's private secretary, James Grigg, wasn't best pleased either. He had to pick up the pieces and he refers to the matter sharply in his memoirs.

All this I was reminded of a few years ago in a casual chat with Lord MacAndrew who, as he also reminded me, happened to be occupying the Chair in the House throughout the whole sad little saga. Charlie MacAndrew also sent me a copy of the *Kilmarnock Standard* for 12 May 1928 (his constituency newspaper) in which he had set the story down as part of his weekly article. His covering note to me said "Leo Amery carted your father" which seems to me a hard but not unjustified verdict.

I had actually heard the story once before from Amery himself. He had come down to Oxford to address the University Conservative Association and he invited me to dine with him in All Souls, purposely, I think, to give me his version of this story.

He told me that he realised he had acted hastily, had apologised to my father and had also told Winston exactly what had happened. Did I know whether Winston had ever made it up with my father? I said I couldn't remember which was not wholly true. I'm pretty certain he never did and that I call unkind.

In contrast, Winston was always extremely kind to me. It's presumptuous to think that he may have had a twinge of conscience about that wretched lighter, but kind he certainly was. He gave my wife and me our first wedding present, two beautifully bound volumes of his life of Marlborough with the modest little inscription "I hope you may be able to find room for these on your shelves." I liked the idea of us finally making up our minds to throw out a few old Penguins and some back numbers of Wisden to make space for Winston and the Duke.

I joined the Churchill government in 1953 in the not outstandingly important role of Under Secretary of State at the Home Office. I once even attended a Cabinet Meeting as stand-in for my S of S when he was struck down with 'flu. However, as I was not called upon to utter a single word, I think I can honestly say that I didn't disgrace myself.

I had a little more to say, though, at Winston's last three general elections when he gave me the task of holding the fort for him at his eve-of-poll meetings. This is an exacting business in any constituency because the fort-holder has to go on talking until the candidate arrives from his previous meeting. I once had to burble on for nearly an hour when Sir Gerald Wills, the candidate for Bridgewater, sustained a puncture in the wilds of Somerset. As I collapsed back into my seat like a punctured accordian, my wife's neighbour turned to her and remarked genially "My word, 'ow 'e do chat!'

Holding the fort for Winston presented a further hazard because one's powerful peroration was invariably drowned by the cheers that greeted the great man as his cavalcade approached the hall.

On another occasion he invited me to address the AGM of his constituency Young Conservatives and disaster nearly overtook that one too. I was winding up a debate for the Government in the Lords and the Whips said it would end in comfortable time for me to get away. Their Lordships, however, proved unusually loquacious and I soon realised I should never get to Woodford in time. My wife, who was coming with me, was listening to the debate from what is irreverently known as the Peeress's Pig-Pen so I passed along to her the notes for my Young Conservative speech and told her she'd have to hustle off and make it for me. Fortunately, she cannot only read my handwriting but can also make a thumping good speech in her own right. All must have gone well, for Winston sent her a charming telegram which, oddly enough, we have kept.

I think, that I also have one of the few Winston stories without words. In 1942 I was serving as a Second Grade Staff Officer in the Military Operations Directorate at the War Office. One of our jobs was to brief the Secretary of State on North African operations with which our branch was particularly concerned. By coincidence the S of S was none other than Sir James Grigg, Winston's former Private Secretary at the Treasury, and I sometimes wondered if he ever realised whose son I was. I didn't, as a matter of fact, think highly of him, either as an MP or as Secretary of State, but I can genuinely say that my opinion was in no way biased by his attitude towards petrol lighters.

Another of our jobs was to go across to Downing Street when the Prime Minister was away and bring his war maps up to date. One Saturday afternoon, I was lying on the ante-room floor, surrounded by chinagraph pencils, talc and dusters, with my hat and belt beside me, looking, I suppose, not unlike a pavement artist in Trafalgar Square. Suddenly Winston, whom I believed to be down at Chequers, bustled into the room chatting volubly to the American General, Omar Bradley. I clambered uneasily to my feet but he waved me down and went on into the Cabinet Room. Just as he got to the door he paused, looked back at me, put his hand into his pocket, took out a penny and without a word threw it into my hat. The penny, like my wife's telegram, has been kept.

What I had not been able to keep was a note of a meeting held at Sir Samuel Hoare's house in Cadogan Gardens on 18th October 1922. About 30 Conservative MP's were present including Sir Arthur Steel-Maitland, an ex-Chief Whip, and Sir Shirley Benn, an ex-Chairman of the National Union, who both gave the impression that they had come to spy. My father was deputed to take a note of the proceedings which he duly did. His own copy was lost in the blitz, but he had prudently placed another copy in the archives of the British Museum whence it has only now passed into the Public Domain. The meeting was in effect a dress rehearsal for the famous Carlton Club meeting of the next day which brought about the downfall of Lloyd-George. That meeting has been frequently described, but this is the first description I myself have read of the gathering at Cadogan Gardens.

I extract the following from my father's note: "Birkenhead and Churchill were described as two of the biggest rogues that have ever been members of a British Cabinet." My father, who spoke first, adds this rider: "I agree about Churchill who is an unprincipled and arrogant gambler with National counters, in the interests of his own fortunes. Birkenhead's main fault is his reputed reckless private life. Churchill is a rogue. Birkenhead is not a rogue though he is on all sides regarded as a loose liver. But I have never seen him do anything wrong. Nevertheless, the known intimate personal friendship existing between Birkenhead and Churchill has long been a source of suspicion to Conservatives who have regarded Birkenhead's friendship with Churchill as having not only an element of disloyalty but as likely to contain the germ of some hanky-panky, should an occasion arise convenient to themselves."

My father died in 1942. I wish he had lived long enough to acclaim a different sort of Churchill. I also wonder whether Churchill ever knew anything about that meeting in Cadogan Gardens.

10
Success

As I grow older I begin to wonder whether success is really all that important. I'm also beginning to wonder whether importance isn't becoming less important too.

Indeed, I'm beginning to share the views of that pugnacious philosopher, the late Mr. W. C. Fields. "If at first you don't succeed," he used to bellow, "try, try again. Then give up. There's no point in making a damn fool of yourself."

The Fields formula would not, however, have appealed to Sir John Donald Alexander Arthur Makgill of Kemback and Brackmont in the county of Fife, who has just laid successful claim to the dormant viscountancy of Oxfuird. The campaign occupied Sir John and his ancestors for no less than 242 years before their endeavours were at last crowned with victory. I can only hope that the Oxfuirds and their supporters have time to enjoy their success in the Peerage before Mr. Michael Foot and his supporters finally succeed in abolishing the House of Lords altogether.

Success, then, would appear to be relative. It's what you want that counts, not what people think you ought to want. Peerages, power, money, sleek foreign cars and even sleeker foreign blondes – these are the accepted trappings of success, but do they also bring happiness?

Money, if it does not bring you happiness, will at least help you to be miserable in comfort. And if money is indicative of success, then Mr. Paul Getty must have been the most successful man of our time though possibly not the happiest. He was seldom seen to smile and when he was, it was held by common consent to be a very disturbing sight. History does not record what expression Mr. Getty assumed when he found himself unplaced in a newspaper competition which he once entered under a *nom de plume* to decide upon the qualifications most required in a potential millionaire.

For Edward VII's financial advisers, success was synonymous with decorations. They collected stars and orders as you and I might collect Green Shield Stamps. But to judge by their photographs, their dispositions actually grew more gloomy as their sashes grew more gaudy.

Towards the end of her career, Mata Hari, the distinguished spy, grew careless and began to make a few mistakes though she had already achieved greater success as a Grande Horizontale than most plump little Dutch girls have any right to expect. But she kept a sense of proportion about her success and she once told one of her clients that what she really enjoyed most was a bottle of iced lager and a good piece of cheese. I feel this news may have unsettled her client.

Success, however, like lager and lovers can also be comparative. Your view of it can depend upon where you sit. Some while ago I published a small book and hoping that this might arouse a little interest in the neighbourhood, I sent it for the favour of a review to the Editor of our local paper, the *South Gloucestershire Herald* with which is incorporated the *Wiltshire Gazette* and *Cirencester Mercury*. The review, when it eventually appeared, was unexciting and consisted of no more than a paraphrase of my publisher's blurb. The headline, however, gave hint of success in a different class. It read simply "South Gloucestershire man writes book."

Success also depends upon whom you're sitting next to. My friend Charlie Cringleford enjoyed (if that be the proper word) a successful military career. Its start, however, was inauspicious. "Lord Cringleford," wrote his C.O. "is an officer whom the troops will follow to their death, whither his optimistic incompetence must inevitably lead them." Charlie went on to win two D.S.O.'s and his C.O. ended up as Commander, South Midlands Area. So in their relative and comparative ways both achieved the success they doubtless deserved.

In my time, I have tried my hand at the Law, the Army, Politics and Commerce. All four pursuits have had one thing in common. Success therein depended largely upon making one's mistakes when nobody was looking. In due course I shall take up a fifth pursuit prompted by the same desire for success with which I stumbled into the other four. I wish to become a successful potterer.

It's not that I dislike work. Far from it. I love work. I can sit and look at it for hours. It's simply that my standards of success are changing. When I was a politician I realised that success usually went to the man who could make the same mistake twice without losing his nerve. At the Bar I realised that the unsuccessful advocate loses cases that he ought to win and only begins to achieve success when he wins cases that rightly ought to be lost. So, in the end, justice probably prevails.

My pottering will be based on lessons such as these. I shall be calm and contemplative. I shall read Gibbon's *Decline and Fall* right through. I shall study the later string quartets of Beethoven. I shall learn to spell. I shall profit from my foresight in laying down a little of Taylor's '64. I shall watch my wife mowing the lawn. Success in pottering to standards such as these requires much concentration.

I may, however, have just enough time left in which to muse gently on my past successes in other fields. Modesty confines my present review to three particular examples.

Some of us (myself excluded) are tempted to throw all our mistakes into a heap and call them our bad luck. This is dishonest. It is equally dishonest to discount the amount that luck may have played in such success as we may have achieved. I will try to be honest.

Two of my three examples are recorded in *Hansard*. The first was my defeat of the Government in their attempt to put two extra stories on to the top of Carlton House Terrace and convert it into a new Foreign Office. I played every card in the pack. I shouted my head off. I lobbied and I conspired. I wrote letters to *The Times* and I appeared on *The World at One*. Luck then placed an ace in my hand. In a debate in the Lords, the Government spokesman dropped an unexpected and damaging brick. Not to worry, he explained; if you stood directly under the building you wouldn't be able to see the two new stories and if you looked at them from out on Horse Guards Parade you'd think they belonged to the building behind. The asinine illogicality of this argument completed my task for me and the plan was finally scrapped. My success was sweet, but perhaps not wholly deserved.

My second example involved the Law. I had ventured to cross swords with the formidable Lord Goddard, then Lord Chief Justice of England. This was over a Bill to alter the Law about speed limits which, as a Home Office Minister, I was piloting through the Lords. Raynor Goddard was fulminating about the serious restrictions this measure might have on the activities of ambulances, fire engines and police cars. With appropriate diffidence, I intervened. Was it possible, I asked, that the Lord Chief Justice might have overlooked the fact that this situation was already covered by section 71 of the Act of 1952? Lord Goddard was clearly taken aback. He humphed and grumped but finally said he would have another look at it.

Later, he wrote me a kindly note. "You were right," he said, "and I was wrong. But don't try it on too often." What he didn't know was that the official who was briefing me had overheard Lord Goddard's clerk discussing the point in the lobby before the debate and so we were properly forewarned. Once again, good luck had contributed to my success.

I don't know what degree of luck enters into my third success. The details are not recorded in *Hansard*. They are, however, to be found at St. Marylebone Town Hall, in the Marriage Register for 8th May 1951.

65

11
QE2

In the spring of 1966 I was invited to join the board of the Cunard Line as Deputy Chairman of their Passenger Division. Although I was aware that the Line was in financial difficulties, I accepted with alacrity. For two reasons (both personal), I was glad of the opportunity to work with this famous company.

First, I had always been interested in the Merchant Marine. When I was at school at Winchester, my friends and I used to bicycle down to Southampton docks on a Saturday afternoon and clamber round as many liners as would allow us on board. There were plenty enough to visit in 1930. In July 1966, however, when I first opened the door of my new office in Cunard's Southampton HQ (which used to be the old South Western Hotel) I noticed a faded photograph on the wall. It had been taken from the same spot upon which I was then standing. It displayed an overall view of the docks with twenty-two passenger liners lying at their berths. I looked out of the window at the same view. I could count five ships only – a clear indication of the effect wrought upon the world's passenger fleets by Sir Frank Whittle's invention of the jet.

In 1930 I think I knew the vital statistics of every passenger liner in the world of 15,000 tons and over. My father always maintained that I was a mine of wholly useless information but in 1966, owing to changed circumstances, that information came in useful.

The second reason for my pleasure at joining Cunard was really one of serendipity – the happy coincidence. In the 1840's my great-grandfather, Michael Samuel, had gone to work for Samuel Cunard, the founder of the Line. They had come together at Richibuctoo on the Miramachi River in New Brunswick (it is sometimes forgotten that Cunard was originally a Canadian and not a British Company) and although my ancestor's role was obviously no more than that of a glorified ADC, master and servant appeared to have hit if off because, when young Michael left Canada to return to his native Norwich, Samuel Cunard gave him a crisp new $20 bill.

My family's archives of this period are scanty. We lost nearly all our papers when the cellar of our London home was flooded during the blitz. I did, however, come across two items which were of particular interest to me in view of my subsequent connection with Cunard.

Michael Samuel was apparently present in Boston upon the arrival of Cunard's first ship *Britannia* on her maiden voyage in 1848. He records in a letter home that the City Fathers presented the Line with a magnificent silver cup. In the course of time the cup went astray and didn't come to light again until 1967 when it suddenly turned up in Bourdon-Smiths, the well-known silver-smith's in Conduit Street. The firm asked if we were interested, and even though it eventually turned out to be one of the most hideous pieces of table-silver I have ever encountered, its historical significance was obvious so we bought it on the spot. We set it up on a table at the entrance to the Columbia Restaurant in the QE 2 where it was greatly admired by everybody except the ste-wards who had to keep it clean.

The other entry which I extracted from my great-grandfather's jumble of papers reveals a less satisfactory situation. Cunard soon developed an immense, valuable but unedifying immigrant trade. What the poor steerage passengers had to put up with beggars description. Try-ing to cook on an open deck in a force 8 gale was not the worst item in their catalogue of miseries. There was, however, little risk of contagious infection, thanks largely to Samuel Cunard's foresight. He told his ADC to see that all embarking immigrants were scrubbed down thoroughly before boarding. As most of these passengers were Liverpool Irish bound for Boston, one can see whence the Irish-Americans may derive some of their anti-British prejudice.

The first task I was allotted on joining Cunard was the co-ordination of the design plans for the new liner eventually to be known as QE2. At that time it was still known as 736 and consisted of a jumble of steel in John Brown's yards on Clydebank.

This was a task after my own heart. I had for long been interested in design and had served for some years on the Council of Industrial Design under the Director-ship of Sir Paul Reilly. He was at Winchester with me and I later had the pleasure of speaking directly after him and thus of congratulating him when he made his maiden speech in the House of Lords.

Two of my former colleagues on the Council had by coincidence already been appointed members of the QE2 design team. Professor Sir Mischa Black designed our synagogue, now the only one in any ship afloat. It was a great success despite the fact that Mischa, as he later confessed, had not himself been to synagogue for thirty years. The other member was the exotic Gaby Schreiber who designed the theatre and many of the first class cabins and never agreed with any suggestion I ventured to make.

The external design of the ship was the responsibility of James Gardner and the co-ordination of the internal designs lay with Denis Lennon. They jointly controlled or tried to control the work of about fifteen tempera-mental geniuses who were usually at daggers drawn with the Naval Architect, our committee and each other.

Some of this potential mayhem was justifiable. I am, for instance, astonished that Michael Inchbald who designed the beautiful Queen's Room (i.e. the first class lounge) has ever spoken to me since. We had provided for a portrait of the Queen to hang on the forward bulkhead but such a portrait would, we began to think, have looked a little incongruous. I then remembered the spectacularly successful portrait bust of the Queen which the Jugoslav sculptor, Oscar Nemon, had done for the wall above the High Table at my own College, Christ Church, Oxford. I persuaded my colleagues to commission such a bust for the Queen's Room instead of the portrait. They agreed. Her Majesty graciously consented to sit though she cannot have realised that Oscar Nemon would restart his work no less than four times. (The final result was fortunately an artistic triumph.) Unhappily, I forgot to tell Michael Inchbald that the whole of his magnificent wooden screen would have to be reconstructed to accommodate the new work. To say he was put out would be an understatement. He came to my office to complain and brought his two children with him in the hope, he explained, that their presence would act as a brake upon his temper. It failed.

James Gardner had his problems, too, mostly about the funnel. The design of the QE2's funnel has been much criticised, I think unfairly. People would have liked a conventional Cunard funnel, red with black bands. Gardner reluctantly designed such a funnel. It was awful. It stuck out like a sore thumb which is, of course, the only thing sore thumbs ever do. Besides which, what we wanted was a funnel which would throw smuts clear of the deck at any speed and on any course, a thing no other ship had hitherto achieved despite some very odd designs. Gardner's final funnel does just that and thereby fulfils the first rule of Industrial Design – suitability for the job.

Despite all these ups and downs, the tact and skill of Gardner and Lennon always prevailed in the end, and when QE2 eventually went into business the *Architectural Review* ungrudgingly described her as one of the handsomest ships afloat.

We received some interesting presentations. When the *Queen Mary* first entered service, Lloyds very kindly gave her a handsome rose bowl for the Captain's table. It was soon stolen. When the *Queen Elizabeth* returned to service after the war, Lloyds also gave her a rose bowl and that, too, was stolen. So when they offered us yet another rose bowl for QE2 we said thank you very much indeed but do you think we could possibly have something less portable? So we settled on a huge figurehead of *Britannia* which now watches over the entrance to the Britannia restaurant. There are not many people left who can carve figureheads but we found a Mr. Charles Moore, a Cornishman, who did a beautiful job on the lady. Unfortunately, figureheads are meant for the prow of a ship which is a cold, wet and windy place and not for a ship's dining-room which is sometimes a bit warmer. Poor old *Britannia* kept on cracking, sometimes in rather embarrassing places. But even if a bit cracked she's still a bonny, buxom piece.

John Brown, the QE's builders, made an interesting contribution to our decorative ensemble. This, too, is to be found in the Britannia Restaurant. It is a very sensuous contemporary work which we referred to knowingly as a Compound Curve in Three Dimensional Form and which to our satisfaction has been varyingly attributed to Henry Moore and Barbara Hepworth. It is actually the wooden mould from which some of the machinery discharges were constructed in John Brown's yard.

We ourselves soon got to know that yard pretty well because we all used to fly up regularly to Glasgow to see how things were coming along. After a while it became painfully clear that things weren't coming along at all, and the reason for this slowing down in the work soon became equally clear. There were no other passenger ships on order in the yard and the men were understandably reluctant to work themselves out of a job.

We walked one afternoon into a passenger cabin upon which work was not weeks but months behind schedule. Four young gentlemen were sitting round a packing case playing poker. I happened to have a small camera in my hand. One young gentleman got up and came across to me. "If you are thinking of taking a picture of us with yon wee camera," he said, "I'll have the whole bluidy ship out in an hour." We went in search of authority to report the matter but all authority had suddenly and mysteriously disappeared.

Pilferage was another serious problem. Rolls of carpet were carried on to the ship, out of another door and into Glasgow's supermarkets without ever being taken off the shoulder. We were losing more electric light bulbs in a week than the ship could possibly use in a year. Straightforward sabotage was becoming increasingly serious. So we regretfully decided that unless QE2 was taken away from Clydebank and down to Southampton for completion she would never be finished at all.

She sailed on her acceptance trials with an army of workmen still aboard. Everything imaginable went wrong and a great else that could hardly be imagined at all. With regret and considerable courage, Cunard's Chairman, Sir Basil Smallpeice, refused to accept delivery. All hell broke loose. The London *Evening News* carried a headline "Ship of Shame" which was reported in most of the world's press. This, of course, did Cunard and the country no noticeable good. But despite the fact that she has continued to be dogged by misfortune, QE2 has proved a popular and profitable ship.

It was intended that she would spend half the year cruising in warm waters and the rest of the year working across the Atlantic in partnership with the CGT's flagship *France*. The French proved tough negotiators but in Paris, at any rate, discussions were made more agreeable by the fact that the last item on the agenda was invariably lunch or dinner in the French Line's private boat on the Seine. This was anything but tough.

During the course of these discussions it became clear to us that not only the *Queen Mary* but also the *Queen Elizabeth* would have to be withdrawn. They had given wonderful service both in peacetime and in war when they had carried over a million American soldiers across to Europe. But they were both getting old, they were guzzling up an immense amount of fuel oil and they were losing money. Although the *Elizabeth* had undergone an extensive refit including the construction of an outdoor swimming pool she really wasn't much more suitable for cruising than the *Mary*.

I was given the disagreeable task of flying out to Cork, boarding the *Mary* and breaking the news to the crew that their ship would be taken out of service in the near future. They accepted philosophically what they must all have known was inevitable.

We eventually sold her to the City of Long Beach in California. Her journey out via the Horn was not a happy one. She was no longer in Cunard's ownership and Captain Treasure Jones told us that she had run out of practically everything especially temper, but the welcome she received as she sailed into Long Beach was heartwarming and spectacular. I visited her several times whilst the City Fathers were converting her into a Convention Centre and Museum of the Sea. I think I should have watched the work with mixed feelings even if she hadn't already been the centre of a blazing row between the Mayor, the Banks, the Insurance Companies and a wide variety of middle-men who had eased themselves into the act.

I myself got into the act on one occasion and that was a mistake. They were trying to repaint the funnels and couldn't get the colour right. I said I wasn't surprised. The exact colour of Cunard Red was our private property but I'd look into the matter when I got back to Southampton. I did. Southampton was not best pleased. They asked if I realised how much paint would be needed, what it would cost, what the freight charges would be and would I please be a bit more careful in future.

When I was out in America, I was wearing two hats; one was Cunard's and the other that of the British National Export Council of whose American Committee I was Chairman. Whilst trying to drum up business for Britain in general I also tried, quite unashamedly, to drum up business for Cunard in particular. It wasn't always easy. I remember going to the offices of Thomas Cook in Atlanta where they were our agents. With much tact, they had laid out a cabin plan of QE2 along the shipping desk. The shipping clerk, a little black girl of about eighteen, gave me a beaming welcome. I thanked her and congratulated her on her enthusiasm and on her enterprise in trying to sell space in a ship she'd never even seen. "Sir," she said, "I've never even seen the sea."

QE2 was, of course, designed with a special eye on the American market. The fact that she could squeeze through the Panama Canal would, we hoped, be a good selling point when we were planning long cruises. Imagine, therefore, our horror when the Hydrography Department of the Admirality came to us and said they were redrawing the charts of the Canal Zone and were pretty certain we'd got our sums wrong and she wouldn't be able to squeeze through at all.

Our Naval Architect and his boys got out their wet towels and their pocket calculators and legged it for Panama. They came back hot and angry. They told us there was nothing wrong with their figures and they went off to repeat this to the Hydrography Department of the Admiralty. Oh yes, said the Admiralty, perhaps there had indeed been some misunderstanding. Maybe they'd been a bit hasty. Sorry. By the time I left Cunard we were still trying to get the Admiralty to repay us for our Naval Architect's ticket to Panama.

Meanwhile, we were preparing to dispose of *Queen Elizabeth*. It was not an easy task, but eventually she was bought by a consortium of entrepreneurs in Philadelphia of whose background, and intentions we had not made ourselves sufficiently aware. The local newspaper, however, was more inquisitive. The *Philadelphia Enquirer* lived up to its name. We had to call the deal off.

We then took the ship down to Fort Lauderdale in Florida and tried again. This time we were more circumspect. We invited the Governor of the State, the Press and all the local big wigs to lunch on board. The Governor made a happy reference to the *Queen Mary* in California and the *Queen Elizabeth* in Florida propping up the United States of America like a couple of gigantic book ends. He also said it would be better if we turned the ship into a company and this we accordingly did.

We were told that we should need a financial adviser at about a million dollars a year, a legal adviser (at ditto), a PR man (ditto ditto) and an adviser on roads. Now look, we said, we're a ship and too big to go along roads. Why on earth should we need an adviser on roads? They told us we were missing the point. Our adviser-to-be on roads was the Governor's father. We said well, yes indeed; we were beginning to understand how business in Florida is conducted. He turned out to be the most useful of all our advisers. We had some interesting offers including one from a Panam captain named Charles Blair who wanted to use her as a casino lying off his private island in the West Indies but he withdrew when he discovered she'd have to anchor nearly 5 miles out.

Eventually the ship was sold to Mr. C. Y. Tung, the Chinese multi-millionaire, who renamed her *Seawise University* (joke) and sailed her out to Hong Kong where she mysteriously caught fire and now lies, a charred and hideous wreck. There are many who think it would have been better to have broken up both the *Mary* and the *Elizabeth* immediately their days were over, and I'm beginning to think they were right.

The last time that I saw the *Elizabeth* she was lying off Aruba waiting for spare parts for her stricken boilers. She was Hong Kong bound and we, in QE2, were on passage for Martinique. We exchanged hail and farewell greetings on our sirens and there wasn't a dry eye in sight.

At Martinique I switched into Cunard's *Carmania* and eventually flew home from Barbados. Ship-hopping is one of the most splendid ways of combining business

with pleasure, particularly for a ship-lover like myself.
Carmania and *Franconia* were two of Cunard's four
twenty thousand tonners, originally built for the
Canada trade, but all too soon to join the ranks of Sir
Frank Whittle's victims. Two of the four were sold
abroad and the other two we rebuilt, with some success,
as cruise liners.

Of necessity, all three ships were away from home for
long periods particularly during the cruising season, and
there was always the risk of Ships' Companies and
Cunard Line Management dropping out of touch with
each other. So we invented ship-hopping. You flew,
say, to Barbados; boarded *Franconia* for Jamaica where
you carted your toothbrush and nightie across to *Carmania* bound for Antigua, and thence via QE2 back to
New York where you could learn from Cunard's chauffeur Albert (the fount of all wisdom) how things were in
the office.

This splendid drill was not confined to the Western
Hemisphere. I stood on the quay in Durban and
watched QE2's captain, the arrogant but able Commo-
dore Bil Warwick, nudge her in with an inch to spare
(which the Harbour Master said couldn't be done), and
then sailed in her for Cape Town where a southeaster
howling down Adderly Street tried to blow us on to the
Union Castle mail-boat. Warwick and four sweating
tug-masters succeeded in keeping us off. And so to Rio
which I had never previously seen. I recommend a brilliant sunrise on QE2's bridge as the best initiation.

It was also the ship's first visit so we gave a party or
two, and a party or two or three was given back. The
British Ambassador (Sir David Hunt) asked us to lunch.
He told me to bring my wife and some of the ship's
officers. I said I had only one wife and she would love to
come but the ship had more than one officer. How
many? Two? Three? Sir David said that he thought
about twelve would do nicely and when we got to the
Embassy we could see why he'd said it. Her Britannic
Majesty's Embassy in Brazil is about the size of Bucking-

ham Palace and was approved by Ernie Bevin, of all people, when he was Foreign Secretary. He said he wasn't going to have any dam dagoes cocking a snook at the British Ambassador. Alas, the Embassy has had to move up to Brazilia, the new capital, which some, but not all, say is a very lovely place.

The smaller ships had their moments too. We took *Carmania* into Montreal for Expo '67 and gave a dinner, no, dammit, a banquet for the VIP's who were attached to the exhibition. I remember that the 2nd purser and my secretary had to escort home several VIP's who had temporarily run into trouble.

On board *Carmania*, in my last year with Cunard, I helped to celebrate St. Patrick's Day. With its Liverpool connections, Cunard still carried a lot of Irish on the crew-decks. St. Patrick's Day celebrations could sometimes end in worry, but not on this occasion. The next morning I encountered the ship's doctor eating an apple and reading a book about butterflies by the swimming-pool. "How did it go last night?" I asked. "Much trouble? Mayhem in the boiler-room and so on?"

"No," he said, taking another bite at his apple. "Not at all. In fact, pitifully quiet. Only four stitches."

One of the unexpected hazards encountered by QE2 was the fact that, being the fastest ship for miles around, she always had to go to the aid of anyone in trouble. This cost us a lot of time, fuel and temper because although everybody was very keen to be rescued, not everybody was quite so keen to pay for the privilege once the rescue was over and done with.

Occasionally a rescue provided interesting sidelights. We took off about 600 passengers from the French Line's *Antilles* when she ran aground near the island of Mustique. Amongst the passengers was an elderly French Grande Dame who was obviously and understandably shaken by her misadventure. We cosseted her as best we could and eventually she was sufficiently recovered to take dinner in the Verandah Grill. Arthur

Townsend, our head chef, put his best foot forward. Madame thanked us prettily but added that she hoped we would not mind if she expressed the view that the sauce Béarnaise was a little bit too thick. Mr. Henley, our normally imperturbable Grill Room manager, was for once abnormally perturbed, and he strode off into the kitchen muttering loudly to himself. "A little bit too thick, indeed! The old cow can say that again."

I recall an occasion that was slightly colder than our entry into Rio Harbour. It was alongside Pier 92 in New York, with several feet of ice in the harbour but no tugs or longshoremen to man the ropes. They were all on strike. Warwick decided to take QE2 in singlehanded, with a few Cunard typists and clerks on the ropes. (This has been done before, but it requires skill. The Italian Line once pushed their *Leonardo da Vinci* half-way along into a nearby streetmarket.)

Bil waved the pilot aside and after sixty minutes of unassisted ice-breaking (which is thirty more than is needed with assistance) we were safely tied up alongside. I thought the pilot looked a little out of countenance and suggested that Bil offer him a consoling word. "Anything I can do for you, Pilot?" he asked, without much warmth. I thought there was going to be an explosion. But no. "Yes, Captain, there is," said the pilot. "I should like a signed copy of the log for my grandchildren."

I had enjoyed my first entry into New York in QE2 on her maiden voyage, with the fire hydrants squirting and the bands playing and Mayor Lindsay climbing aboard, but I think I enjoyed this icy entry even more.

Two frequent passengers in QE2 were the brothers Hinkley who were the directors of an American charter airline named Overseas National Airlines. They planned to enter the cruise business themselves and had two 15,000 tonners on the stocks in Rotterdam. They walked for hours round QE2, pencil and paper in hand, seeking to profit from our experience.

Suddenly the US Government clamped down and

forbade an American airline to operate passenger ships. After much complicated negotiation, Cunard took the two ships over from ONA and they became the *Cunard Adventurer* and the *Cunard Ambassador*. I myself wanted them to be given the two distinguished old Cunard names of *Aquitania* and *Berengaria*, and though I was in a surly minority of one, I still think I was right.

We used to go across regularly to the Rotterdam Dry Dock and the Smit yards to see how the two ships were coming along, and I'm sorry to have to say that they came along much more punctually than the QE2 did at Clydebank.

My wife launched the *Adventurer* but we never had the pleasure of sailing in her. The Cunard Company was taken over before the ship was put into commission.

I went down to Southampton to say goodbye to QE2 which for five years had played a major part in my life. Bil Warwick gave me my usual pink gin and discussed the Test Match. He came out of Cunard shortly after I did. I happened to be looking for a secretary for the Appeal Fund of St. George's Hospital of which I was Chairman. I'm glad to say he was able to accept my invitation.

The Staff of the Midship's Bar gave me a set of steward's buttons for my blazer. They said the plain ones I usually wore didn't look quite right.

The master-at-arms shook me by the hand as I stepped ashore. "May I ask you a question?" he said. (Lord knows what would have happened if I'd said no. You don't argue with an ex-RSM of the Royal Marines.) "I suppose most people like you have a mistress?" "Well, that's as may be," I replied guardedly. "In which case," he went on, "you must be the only person I've ever met who's got a mistress with a steel bottom."

I looked back at QE2's lovely long sleak lines and blew my nose loudly.

12

A Chinaman in my Bath

I'm afraid the business orgy is dying out. Round about
10.30 am on the third Wednesday in every month the
tea-lady comes into our boardroom, and puts in front of
my colleagues the cup of iron filings boiled in tannic
acid which they all seem to like. In front of me, however, she sets a pot of Lapsang Suchong China tea, and
this, I fear, my colleagues regard as epicene, if not down-
right decadent, though they are too polite to say so. And
that's about as near to an orgy as we ever get in our corner
of E.C.4.

Studying, however, as I do, all these stories in the
New of the World about sales reps whooping it up in
Walthamstow, and the Bacchanalian revels that seem to
go on after hours in Throgmorton Street, I'm beginning
to wonder whether our board isn't missing something.

We have our usual Christmas party in the office, of
course, and very enjoyable it is, too. I notice, however,
that some companies are dropping this particular celeb-
ration. I suppose they feel that there's a risk of an unre-
flective little frippet from Accounts saying something to
the managing director late in the evening which may
unbalance the office for weeks to come.

One of our contractors, for instance, tells me that
their office party last Christmas was disturbed by a
young lady from the typing pool. She rushed into the
general office observing, "I've been seduced." Her
friends crowded round to give her comfort. "Who
could have done this dastardly thing?" they inquired.
"Obviously one of the directors," she replied. "Who
else would wear an Old Etonian tie, and make me do all

79

the work?"

Business, of course, has been business down the ages, but somehow I think our forebears managed to mix business and pleasure with greater panache than we do. Take the Romans. Petronius has a nice bit in *The Satyricon* about a dinner party given by a neighbour who wanted to acquire a few acres off him at a knock down price. History doesn't relate how the deal went, but it does record that the host kindly provided a little golden-haired slaveboy through whose curls the guests could run their fingers when they had got a bit greasy from the Umbrian chicken legs and ham bones. Now, that's really obliging. I doubt if you could get that sort of service in the Savoy even if you gave them weeks of notice.

Plautus had sensible views, too. In one of his plays he demonstrates that the best way to crack an egg is to place it between the navels of two young Nubian slavegirls standing face to face, and then instruct them to rotate simultaneously. But suppose you are taking out a couple of tough Dutch shipbuilders to lunch at the Ecu de France, you can't just send down to the Brook Street Bureau and ask if they've got a couple of Nubian egg-crackers on the books. They'd have you round at the Savile Row police station in a trice.

And what about the Rape of the Sabine Women? That sort of behaviour wouldn't go down at an English party even in this Permissive Age. Imagine if you were asked to the Ladies Night at the local Rotary Club, and just as they were tucking into the Bombe Surprise you suddenly scooped up all the wives of the Committee, popped them over the bonnet of the Rover, and away home you went to Potters Bar. Well, I mean, you wouldn't be asked again, would you?

I'm beginning to think that the whole of this Wine, Women and Song stuff is a bit exaggerated as far as British business is concerned. About American business I'm not so sure. What usually happens in fact is that you are taken out to the Tycoons' Club for luncheon to celebrate the deal. To a background of gin and Musak, you're given far tee many Martoonis. You're then treated to a piece of steak the size of the West Riding of Yorkshire (and about as yielding) which you wash down with scalding hot, white, very sweet coffee, and after you've gone down in an elevator which leaves your stomach up on the top floor, you stagger out into Wall Street and send off a Telex to your chairman saying the deal has been clinched, to which he replies, sourly, "Why only three per cent?"

These are the facts. But in legend, i.e., in *Playboy* magazine, things turn out differently. The boys take you out to dine in Greenwich Village, and shortly after the Pot Roast has been done with, the Maître D wheels in an enormous cake out of which erupts 38-26-38 of very undressed blonde who raises her glass in a bumper toast to the Discounted Cash Flow. This is an entertainment at which I have never actually assisted.

I must confess that I did once go to a Travel Sales Conference at the Coventry Street Corner House where a lady named Princess Ouida Ouigglebelli (or something like that) had been engaged to take off all her clothes slowly and quietly to music. The guests on either side of me expressed the opinion that she was a nice enough girl, though she was constructed on architectural principles too generous for their taste, and that next year they would prefer Morecambe and Wise. I, too, was beginning to wonder whether business and sex really mix.

My Uncle Percy used to drop dark hints about celebrating a successful coup by taking some charming little thing out to supper in a private room at Rules, and drinking champagne out of her slipper. Even if he did, I believe the operation must have been a great deal more complicated than it sounds. And knowing my Uncle Percy, I bet he made a right mess of it, too. The nearest I've ever been to it myself was during the war when I went to a Hogmanay Party with the London Scottish, where they were reduced to drinking oatmeal stout out of a NAAFI girl's gumboot. The experiment was not a success.

The Russians, of course, have to be different. In their funny Victorian way they still foster the idea of the tired Western businessman relaxing to the sound of throbbing balalaikas whilst the current Mata Hari adjusts the bugging device behind the armoire.

Some while ago I went to Leningrad with a deputation from the British Tourist Authority. On the first night after our arrival the Russian Travel boys threw a party in our honour. It was a fine party (they wanted a good deal from us) and by midnight we were awash in vodka. Knowing that I had to make a speech next day I slipped away to my room, undressed, and went into the bathroom in search of Alka Seltzer. Slightly to my surprise I found an elderly Chinaman sitting in my bath washing his toes. "Hi," I said loudly (in English, of course). To which he replied, "Hi," equally loudly in Chinese, which, in these circumstances, sounds roughly the same. I put on my dressing-gown, and in some confusion ran out into the corridor, and into the welcome arms of my colleagues Lord Geddes and Sir Charles Forte. They led me back to my room explaining comfortingly that I was not drunk but had merely forgotten that in the Astoria Hotel, Leningrad, each bathroom served two bedrooms, and that unless you also locked the other door from the inside you were bound to find someone like an elderly Chinaman in your bath. Relieved, I retired to bed, and slept the sleep of the just.

But at breakfast time next morning our interpreter, Tanya, bore down upon us with lowering brow. We asked anxiously if ought was amiss. Indeed there was. As a matter of fact there has been a diplomatic *crise*; a *démarche*, even. It appeared that the Deputy Chairman of the Soil Erosion Committee of the People's Republic of Outer Mongolia had been insulted in his bath by an Alcoholic Nude.

My friends tutted an anxious tut, but loyally did not give me away. I'm sorry to say that I sat silent in smug

content. There could be few international Travel Con-
ferences, I felt, that had ever been addressed by an
Alcoholic Nude, and a member of the House of Lords at
that.

13
More means less

Apparently we've been having a drought down in our part of Gloucestershire. I didn't realise this until I received a note from the Coln Valley Water Board asking me not to water the lawn. I stopped watering the lawn and went round to see the Coln Valley Water Board. I explained to them that I didn't want to water the lawn when it was raining but only when the lawn was dry and turning brown up by the woodshed. I gave them a brief paraphrase of the passage in Adam Smith's *Wealth of Nations* about the law of supply and demand and the relationship between Glut and Shortage. I felt that this would surely make the Board see reason.

The Coln Valley Water Board said yes indeed of course and thank you very much but would I please stop watering the lawn because it was causing trouble up at the pumping station. As I walked home, it started to rain and it's been raining pretty steadily ever since. A lot of guttering has come down and our woodshed is in the middle of a sizeable lagoon.

I rang up Mr. Hodges, the plumber, to ask for help. Mrs. Hodges answered the 'phone and said no she was sorry, Jim wouldn't be able to come round for some time; he had a lot of work on hand; you'd no idea the number of lagoons there'd sprung up in our part of Gloucestershire and what a pity I hadn't rung him up last week when things were dryer.

Nye Bevan would have been interested in all this. Some years ago we had a serious shortage of coal and fish. Nye pointed out that this country was built on coal and surrounded by fish and only an organising genius could contrive a shortage of both at the same time. He had a point.

Nye was also fond of a drop of claret. Until quite recently there has been a serious shortage of fine claret and even quite important drinkers were facing the prospect of downing Château Plonque for the rest of their lives. Now, all of a sudden, it seems that a magnum of the 1971 Haut-Paradis (for drinking in about 1978) can once again be picked up for a pittance. On the other hand there's a shortage of sugar, a glut of beef and the loo-paper market is in sorry disarray. They're importing coal into Cardiff whence they used to export it by the shipload; and wheat into Kenya, though this may have something to do with the fact that the efficient Africans now run the estates hitherto owned by the incompetent British. Adam Smith, thou shouldst be living now.

Actually, it's all the fault of ecology. You have, say, a plague of boll-weevils (*anthonomus grandis*) in Bournemouth. So the clever chemists come up with a non-polar carbon tetrachloride which puts paid to the boll-weevils. But the diet of the boll-weevil (apart from the boll) is principally the platyhelminth flatworm. So, do away with the boll-weevil and what do you get? A glut of flatworms in Bournemouth. Game, set and match to Mother Nature.

Full tribute to this inexorable sequence of glut and shortage is paid, quaintly enough, in our Royal Coat of Arms. Don't deceive yourself that those splendid animals, desporting themselves all over the place, rampant, passant and even sejent guardant are lions. They're nothing of the sort. They're cats. And this is because, in days gone by, the country's prosperity was based on wool. Cats eat mice. Mice eat bees. Bees fertilise the clover which feeds the sheep who give us lovely wool not to mention lovely mutton-chops. Shortage of cats, shortage of wool. Glut of cats, lots of wool. Prosperity. It's as simple as that.

This sequence, mark you, started a long time before

the cat/sheep syndrome. There's nothing new about glut and shortage. What about Pharaoh and the seven fat years of wheat and the seven lean years and the seven fat kine eating up the seven lean kine (ugh!). What about that glut of milk and honey which must have made a nice change for the Children of Israel, doing as best they could on manna and stringy little Gippy quails? Even so, a glut of milk and a shortage of honey at the same time would have produced an admin. problem to baffle even such a competent Q. officer as Moses. Moses could have made good use of our Bombardier Bean. When we set sail for Normandy in June 1944 a generous High Command allotted us one jeep for the whole of our HQ. We filled it with petrol, ammunition and self-heating soup. "Petrol?" said Bombardier Bean, "We must be out of our minds. When we get to the other side we'll be able to borrow petrol from our neighbours or knock it out of the Germans. If we can't do that, it'll mean we've lost the war. Let's take out the petrol and put in bread. Nobody else'll have that."

And so it was. There was a glut of petrol and a great shortage of bread. Bread became currency and we all became very rich. Bombardier Bean, seeking female company one night, went into Bayeux with a loaf of Hovis under his arm.

He came back next morning with a satisfied smirk on his face and six eggs and a Camembert cheese in his hands by way of change.

I should have welcomed his company and his comments when Mr. Hodges eventually came to readjust our lagoon. Some months ago we decided to install a mushroom bed down behind the rose-garden. We bought costly humus and spore, studied all the textbooks, watered and manured, watched and prayed. Nothing happened. Eventually, in disgust, we dug up the mushroom bed and chucked it into the woodshed, replacing it with delphiniums.

When Mr. Hodges eventually arrived to give judgement on the lagoon he thought he'd better have a look in the woodshed. I went with him. It was knee-deep in mushrooms.

14
My next Yacht

My next yacht is going to be much bigger than my last. Actually there was some doubt in the upper echelons of the Bembridge Sailing Club as to whether a scruffy secondhand dinghy named *The Crab* ought to have been classed as a yacht at all.

In other respects, too, her debut had been inauspicious. The very day we acquired her she slipped her moorings, and, without any help from us, ran away to sea. The Coastguards apprehended her in the nick of time, and this was just as well because when Harry Hulbert's boat broke loose the previous week it ended up on the beach at Ostend, and Harry had to apply for an import licence to get her back. It was apparently thought that her return unlicensed might have prejudiced the British boat-building industry.

A contrite *Crab* was duly restored to us. We loaded her with thermos flasks, Norwich terriers, and other essential gear, and set course for Itchenor. Five minutes and two cable lengths later we rammed Lord Brabazon full amidships in *Tara*, and this was an encounter which not even the *Queen Mary* would have undertaken with impunity.

Lord B. of T. was very nice about it. Well, fairly nice. It was generally understood, he reminded us, that the two most useless things in a small boat were an umbrella and a Naval Officer. But now (looking pointedly at me) he had a third candidate to put forward. And, in any case, what was that I had on my head?

He was referring, I supposed, to my new green woollen pom-pom hat. I had bought it specially for the Bembridge Regatta, which is always a very pukka affair. Rear-Commodores and others stride around wearing white-topped caps and purposeful expressions. To appear amongst them bare-headed would, I felt, be inadequate, and to wear a white-topped cap would have been above my station. I suspected, however, that I must have misjudged the situation when the Bembridge policeman came into the Club and complained that the entrance was being blocked by a Rover car owned by a gentleman wearing a green woollen pom-pom hat. Clifton, our steward, replied sharply that no gentleman would ever wear a green woollen pom-pom hat. Apart from this, the Bembridge folk were extremely kind, and I enjoyed my membership of their Club. Indeed, I find that my banker's order is still in existence even though I left the Island many years ago.

I'm afraid, however, that I cannot agree with Ratty that there is nothing, absolutely nothing, better than simply messing about in boats. There is. Yachts, for instance – great big 100-footers, with six double bedrooms and colour TV. I could mess about in them for ever.

Of course, there is a wide range of alternatives between *The Crab* and a 100-footer, and I have considered them all.

We don't want to get involved in anything like hard work; no blistered palms; no salt spray whipping through the hair, nor any nonsense like that. Mr. Heath has not actually invited me to join the crew of his *Morning Cloud*, but if he were to do so I should have to decline. I am, however, comforted to read that you can disregard any of his orders as long as you say "Sir" at the end of your speech of resignation.

I have always thought that to own a racing yacht would be tantamount to tearing up five pound notes under a cold shower. Mr. Heath, however, is reported to have described *Morning Cloud* as a "bloody good investment". If so, it must be the first yacht to qualify as an investment since Noah built the *Ark*.

No round-the-world single-handed stuff, either. I am enchanted with my own company, but not when I'm being seasick.

A three-ton cabin cruiser? How many does that sleep in comfort? None. And what happens if you're cooped up with a lot of dear friends whom you find you loathe and you aren't due back until Wednesday week?

This happened once to the late and sadly missed Lord Stanley of Alderley. He signed on an earnest young Welsh engineer as a deck-hand. Unhappily they fell out, and Ed Stanley berated him so soundly that the poor fellow threatened to put the matter into the hands of his solicitor as soon as they made Cornwall. "You may," said Ed calmly "put the matter into the hands of your solicitor, or into any other portion of his anatomy which your ingenuity or his forebearance will permit." As soon, however, as they had tied up at Pendragon Creek the young man rushed to the 'phone box to tell his lawyer what had happened. With such Celtic volubility was he doing this that he failed to notice Ed creeping up behind him with a tool kit, and screwing him into the phone box. The boy was soon released because he had only to dial 999, or whatever it is you dial when an eccentric Peer of the Realm has immured you in a Cornish phone box. But the episode caused comment round Pendragon for quite some time to come.

So nothing cribbed, cabinned and confined for me. I shall acquire a yacht that'll make that little job of the late A. Onassis look like a Connemara coracle.

I shan't worry about the cost, because Mr. J. Pierpont Morgan tells me that if I have to worry about the cost of a yacht I obviously can't afford one. I shan't, of course, be paying British taxes, because I shall be permanently tied up in Portofino or Antibes. This, after all, is the principal reason for owning a yacht. I have never heard of anybody owning a 100-footer that regularly put to sea.

The Hohenzollerns and the Hapsburgs did not own

yachts in order to go anywhere. They merely wanted to wipe the eye of the Czar, the Khedive, and King Edward VII.

I shall lack for nothing. Henri Sartori will be my private chef. The Amadeus String Quartet will play Mozart on the poop-deck. There will be lashings of caviare, and Charles Heidsieck Blanc de Blancs, and I must remember to find out what is the decimalised version of a lashing in case anything runs out. The Misses Taylor, Loren, Bardot, Lollobrigida, Ege and Welch will be my constant guests, and *The Financial Times* will arrive by air each morning. Bliss.

On second thoughts I shall have to put to sea once a year in order to avoid getting stuck for the local rates. I shall, of course, fly a flag of convenience so that I can't be held responsible if I get the charts upside down, and collide with somebody in the Channel. Whither shall I sail? Why, Bembridge, of course, though I shan't be able to get into the Harbour. Thanks to British Rail this is now silting up. I shall therefore have no problem with British yacht tonnage. This is calculated on the amount of square foot of deck open to the sun, and you have to pay about £1 a ton every time you enter harbour.

It's a very complicated calculation. One of the chaps at the Admiralty, whose job it was to do it, eventually went mad and designed a yacht of such extraordinary proportions that its tonnage worked out at minus seven. He then sailed it all round Britain demanding £7 off the harbour-master at every port of call.

I shall hope to arrive off Bembridge in time for their annual Regatta, where the presence of my yacht may help to discountenance their uppity neighbours at Cowes. I shall, of course, say nothing about that banker's order. I shall just stand on the bridge, and touch my hat cordially to all my old friends as they sail past. And the hat, I need hardly add, will be green, woollen, and pom-pommed.

15

Evil Communications

Evil communications, as St. Paul sternly warned the Corinthians, corrupt good manners. History does not relate whether the Corinthians ever bothered to answer the great man's two epistles. I suspect that they just sighed in resignation, put them in the pending tray and went on communicating evilly. And this behaviour would have been discourteous even if St. Paul hadn't written some of the finest prose in the English language, because the Apostle was undoubtedly right.

He might even have gone further and added that evil communications not only corrupt good manners; they also corrupt industrial relations, politics, married life and a good cash-flow.

How often, for instance, have we not been told that a strike or some other commercial upheaval has been brought about by a breakdown in communications? Frankly, I seldom believe it. I suspect that there weren't any communications to break down in the first place.

I always think it odd that three of the subjects in which we seldom receive instruction at any stage of our education are Parenthood, Citizenship and Communications. People seem to think that these important and complex subjects come to us naturally. This is not so. Like bicycling, swimming or sex they are seldom forgotten once they have been learnt, but learnt they have to be.

Demosthenes, for instance, walked up and down the beach talking to himself with his mouth full of pebbles to improve his diction; Cicero harangued empty benches in the Senate and Winston Churchill used to strike out all the adverbs of his finished articles in order to sharpen their impact. So don't let any of us be too proud to look to our own technique in the field of communications and the field is big enough in all conscience.

It extends, for instance, further than the M4, Concorde and QE2 though they, of course, are communications at their most basic. For businessmen like myself, the Media must also be mastered if we are to make any impact outside our office walls. The word Media, like most vogue words, is imprecise in its meaning. It embraces Press, Radio, TV and the Soap-box. Politicians use all these means of communicating and some of them have gone to considerable lengths to learn the tricks of the trade. A few of them have even learned the trade as well as the tricks. But listen in to Radio 4 of a morning and see whether you think that the broadcast of business in the House enhances your respect for Parliament or not.

Next time you go to Church consider also the Pulpit and the task of its occupant in one of the most difficult of all the functions of communication. Do all our Judges and Magistrates realise the damage that a flippant aside can do to the communication of respect for the Rule of Law?

Consider also communications in the world of Banking in which I am myself engaged. Do they matter and where do we first come across them? Well, to begin with, half the tills close at the busiest time of day and the other half manned by grumpy and disinterested tellers do little to communicate good will between Bank and Customer. Nor does the Bank deserve increased business from the Manager who makes an interview with any but the most prestigious customer seem like a privilege rather than a right. Fortunately, many Banks have grasped these complicated facts and much ingenuity has been lavished on the needs of the humble but regular customer who only wants to pay in a cheque or draw out a modest amount of petty cash. Some communications can be very worthwhile even if they are only petty and modest.

But let's go back to the Manager and, if possible, above him. The day-to-day communications of most businessmen revolve round the telephone, the letter, the memorandum, the interview and the conference. How many of us have learned to make proper use of them?

President Eisenhower, a splendid but not a naturally coherent man, used to complain that he was mis-represented by the Press. The Washington Press Corps (one of the most experienced in the Free World) eventually got tired of this and said, all right, Mr. President, next time we'll write down exactly what you've said without changing so much as a comma. And so they did. When Ike eventually read the speech and noted all the ums and ers and split infinitives and missing verbs, he decided to think out his remarks more carefully in future and put less blame on the Media.

How many of us fall into the same trap and forget that messy communications can sometimes do more damage than no communications at all? How many of us give no thought to the letters we propose to dictate and rely upon our Secretaries to knock our gob-bledegook into something like English? How many of us even bother to read our letters through before we sign them? Failure to do so is a rich source of confused communications.

Next time you receive an incomprehensible letter from your Butcher, Baker or Candlestickmaker tell the good man that in the Peugeot Head Office, in France, the General Manager sticks up on a notice board any memorandum which has come to his attention that is not crystal clear to everybody it is intended to reach.

We Bankers aren't the only offenders. We had a note the other day from our principal American associates. Their unit trust Manager, who had put all his funds into shares rather than keeping some of the money in the Bank, explained this by saying that he was in a 100 per cent investment situation. He had done this, he explained, because the Bank's broker was currently in an investment advisory position. (We thought they couldn't have come to this arrangement over the telephone. They must have indulged in what the Americans call an interfacial involvement.)

Mark you, the telephone which is the most frequently used of all forms of business communication, can throw up some pretty rich gobbledegook when it sets its mind to it. How many of us actually think out an important call before we make it? How many of us are actually at our desks, with our notes readily to hand, when the call eventually comes through, and why do detectives in TV dramas never get as many wrong numbers as I do?

The telephone is an invaluable but very expensive form of communicating but our phone bill would be infinitely smaller if only some of us learned to use the contraption correctly. Incidentally, next time you're at any Head Office, creep quietly down the Executive Corridor and count how many secretaries are engaged in telephoning their boy-friends at the firm's expense and whilst you're about it, you might also ask yourself how many secretaries in how many firms are vital to the business or are merely status symbols helping to communicate their boss's ego.

When I was with the Cunard Line, I remember being shown round the NYK's shipping offices in Yokohama. In many ways, the Japanese communication problems are different from ours, and not only because very little of the rest of the world speaks Japanese.

To begin with, their chain of command is patriarchal. If you're prepared to stick to the rules, you're in the firm till death do you part. The boss, therefore, really is the boss and he's got to know how to communicate right down the line. If the office boy doesn't understand what's going on, it's not his fault; it's the fault of the system.

Japanese executives, however, have to earn their keep. When they are coming up to Board level, they have to pass a test in public speaking. They also have to prove their ability to explain a complex new situation not only to their executive colleagues but also to the workers. They also have to be able to hold a Press Conference and make an impromptu broadcast. I gathered that it didn't matter what they said as long as they were able to say it.

Here at home, we're coming to roughly the same conclusions. We now hold seminars, lectures, teach-ins and courses on all aspects of communications though it's regrettable how often it's only the second eleven who are given time off to attend. The same criticism, I'm afraid, could be levelled at some of the instructors.

As a matter of interest, have a look at the next TV panel which has been assembled to discuss some important managerial problem. In charge, you will find the statutory Chairman – usually an economics don from Redbrick University – genial, fair-minded and slightly out of touch with realities. On his left is an up-and-coming Trade Union official – fluent, persuasive and sticking strictly to the phrase-book. On his right is an up-and-coming Managing-Director, putting a good case with embarrassing incoherence. Why such a difference? Well, the Trade Unionist has probably been talking the hind-leg off a donkey since he was first appointed an Assistant Branch Secretary twenty years ago. That's what he was appointed to do and if he didn't pull it off, the members would think he wasn't worth paying and he'd lose his job. As for the Managing-Director, however, I'd be surprised if he'd been given the chance to address an important meeting until he was well over 30.

I'm beginning to think that the opportunity of learning how to communicate in business is still left too much to chance. But now another chance presents itself.

For better or worse, we are in the Common Market. Whether the French like it or not, the language of the Market will soon be the English language. Until then, we are faced with yet another problem of commercial communications – the problem of using an interpreter and how many businessmen have yet learned to do that?

Have you, for instance, discovered the necessity of taking the interpreter aside before your meeting, letting him get used to your voice and vocabulary, making sure he understands your immediate problem and is learning your own particular idiosyncrasies?

If you haven't, stand by for a communication shambles and then turn on your TV and watch how the job is done by a real expert, such as, for instance, the Queen.

I wonder if St. Paul was using an interpreter when he was reading the riot act to the Corinthians, the Thessalonians and the Ephesians? And I wonder how he would have re-acted if we told him that we have now discovered that the Authorised Version of the Bible had got it all wrong? The new translations say that he didn't mean that evil communications corrupt good manners at all. What he actually said, in his fluent Greek, was that bad company is the ruin of good character.

Let us all think about that next time we're looking round our Board-room table.

16
Booking the Cooks

They have now reconstituted Euston Station and I don't like it at all. I miss the mock-Doric arch and the Victorian grandeur, the sweeping vistas and the Piranesian gloom. They've done away with the train-spotters, those young men who eagerly watched the engines. There used to be another group of men who also watched the engines but with a good deal less enthusiasm. They were called porters – and British Rail seem to have done away with them as well.

Today, Euston is all very functional and hygienic and I miss the echoing transepts and the smoke-encrusted nave. I also missed the 8.30 train to Liverpool but this was hardly the fault of British Rail. My taxi-driver just couldn't find the new front door and who's to blame the man.

So, having a little time to spare, I went off to visit the scene of an event upon which I look back with some quiet satisfaction. This occurred in October 1939 at the Left Luggage office of the Station. The office lies at the end of Platform One, about half way to Manchester.

Lay, alas, not lies. They seem to have pulled the office down in the process of reconstitution and they didn't even leave a little round blue plaque to mark the time and place. Admittedly, it would have been difficult to cram into a few succinct and lapidary words an accurate description of what occurred on the momentous occasion to which I now refer.

In October 1939 the 2nd London Division, into which I had been newly commissioned after several carefree years in the ranks, was ordered to bring itself up to War

Establishment. This involved the mustering and enlistment of about 4,000 conscripts and the subsequent allocation of these reluctant heroes to our various regiments billeted in the Home Counties area round about North London.

Euston Station, in general, and the left luggage office, in particular, were designated as the Divisional Intake Centre. I, for some reason that I never quite understood and my brother officers never understood at all, was appointed Adjutant of this Centre and Frank Lawton, the distinguished actor, was appointed my assistant.

What Frank and I knew about running a Divisional Intake Centre could have been put into a nutshell while still leaving ample room for the nut, but the chaos we accidentally created was not actually as great as my brother officers had feared. What we achieved on purpose is quite a different story.

The War Office had prepared the ground surprisingly well. The nominal rolls were accurate and the cannon fodder arrived roughly as and when expected. All Frank and I had to do was to swear them in, allocate them as appropriate between the regiments, tell Sgt. Meadows to give them a haversack ration and a travel warrant and then pop them into any convenient train – fifty-eight brave men for the London Scottish who lived up by ye banks and braes o' bonnie Rickmansworth, and forty or so for the Ulsters who were out where the mountains of Watford sweep down to the A413.

Just before the boys began to arrive I noticed something rather interesting. Not only did the nominal rolls give the recruit's trade or occupation but they gave it in some considerable detail. They didn't just say "Bill Buggins, Butcher or Baker or Candlestickmaker", they went on to add "Head Butcher at the Marble Arch Corner House", or "Chief Baker at the Savoy". Now it so happened that my own regiment was pretty well off for butchers and bakers and, though I wasn't properly briefed about candlestickmakers, and was therefore prepared to let that matter ride, I knew there were certain key men we did lack and it was at this juncture that I suddenly saw a great light. My brain waved and in next to no time I had flipped through the list and had posted to my own regiment all the best men I could find, including the first trumpeter from the band of the London Palladium, a fish cook from Pruniers, a cutter from Hector Powe, two fitters from Thrupp & Maberly the coachbuilders, a master carpenter from Maples and twenty-six other good men and true who would obviously make life a great deal easier for us in the 117th Field Regt RA. To keep Frank quiet, I also posted some useful stuff to his Greenjackets but all the other regiments just had to take pot luck. We got all the gravy.

At the end of the first day, by which time we had disposed of about a third of our intake, I rang up my brother officers and told them what I had done. They seemed uneasy but pleased and they passed the information on to our Battery Commander who was (and still is) a very nice man. He, too, seemed pleased. "Well done, that man," he remarked in kindly tones. (I think I was only addressed in such terms by a superior officer on two occasions during the whole war and this was both of them – the first and the last.)

When they discovered what had happened (and my ability to cover my tracks was as yet a bit slapdash), the other regiments in the Division were not pleased at all. Not to put too fine a point on it, they raised Hell. Prominent among the Hellraisers were our next door neighbours, a Sapper Field Squadron, with whom we were already on crusty terms as a result of their belief that our Provost Sgt. had deliberately directed their Muscovy ducks into our cookhouse. We particularly disliked their CO. The philosopher Hobbes in his *Leviathan* describes the life of the Elizabethan poor as nasty, brutish and short and this was also an accurate description of the Sappers' Commanding Officer. He had a navy blue face and his moustache grew at right angles to it. He also had a shrewd idea of what had happened at Euston on the previous day and he reported his deductions in some detail to Divisional HQ.

In due course, we received a pretty peremptory order from no less an officer than the AA and QMG. There was to be no more rigging of the lists and no more cooking of the books. All trades were to be fairly and evenly allocated throughout the Division. Was that perfectly clear? Yes, sir.

"We're beaten," said Frank, but I wasn't quite so sure. We got to work on the second day's allocation. Everything was strictly kosher. Here a cook, there a cook, everywhere a fish-cook. I showed Frank the list of trades that I had allocated to those wretched Sappers. All Sir Garnet? Certainly. No jiggery-pokery or lunkleschmunkle? Indeed, no. Then I showed him the men's names and it was here I think, though I say it myself, that I had displayed a certain flair.

London is a cosmopolitan, even a polyglot city. We had by 1939, and before the Immigration Acts, gathered within our hospitable walls men from every country and from all corners of the earth. Some had anglicised their names, but many had not, and this fact was clearly demonstrated by the names of the men I was dispatching to the 201st Field Squadron RE. They were to have a waiter from the Acropolis restaurant named Papadopoulos, a curry cook from the Taj Mahal named Komarakulna'nagara, a solicitor's clerk named Ehrenbreitstein and a swimming instructor named Woisikowski. There were sixteen other such names and the thought of the chaos that would arise in the Squadron office when the SQMS was trying to get out a nominal roll for cookhouse fatigue or, better still, the thought of the RSM trying to get his tongue round that lot when he was calling out the names on Church Parade sent us to bed with a quiet smile playing about our lips.

It came off our lips pretty smartly on the following Monday morning. My brother officers telephoned and warned me that the weekend had not been without incident. The atmosphere at Divisional HQ was, to say the least of it, lively. The matter had even been referred to

Beds and Herts Sub-Area. I might expect a visitation from on high and in some strength at any minute. "Frank," I said, "I'm afraid we're in trouble." "Where do you get the *we* from?" asked Frank peevishly, "You're the brain-box who thought this scheme up, you jolly well think it down again."

I had no time to cudgel my brains before Sgt. Meadows put his head round the door. "Like what I thought, gentlemen," he observed sadly. "We got bov-ver." He was right, too. Platform One was knee-deep in Brigadiers and they were all heading our way.

I will draw a veil over the next few minutes which were, like the Sapper CO, nasty, brutish and short. The leading Brigadier began by casting serious doubt on the authenticity of my parents' marriage lines and went on to express misgivings about my prospects of salvation in the world to come. It wasn't just the enormity of what I had done that was riling Higher Authority, it was the fact that the War Office scheme was so elaborately contrived that, once a man had been posted to a specific unit, it was almost impossible to get him unposted. I must confess that the thought of a poor little Burmese cobbler named, I think, U Nut, having to spend the whole of his war with those nasty, brutish Sappers wor-ried me and made me wonder whether I might not have gone just a little bit too far.

Although it may have been too late to unravel the mischief I had wrought, there were still a thousand or so men to be posted. From now on, however, the rules were to be scrupulously observed. Was this understood? Was it clear what would happen to me if the rules were once again unobserved? I had been standing to attention for about twenty minutes and was beginning to get the message. The Brigadiers withdrew. Wearily we returned to our proformae. We were down but not, it suddenly dawned on me, out.

For an hour I sweated away on the last of the men for the 201st Field Squadron. It proved to be my finest hour. I handed my list to my colleagues. Frank Lawton and Sgt Meadows went through it with knitted brows. At first blush it was faultless. The Butchers, Bakers and Candlestickmakers were all immaculately balanced. There were no funny names at all. But suddenly it dawned upon them also what I had achieved and they flashed upon me a gratifying smile of appreciation which, as the full implications of my plan sank in, widened until they were looking at me like a nun looking at a Cardinal.

I had posted to the 201st Field Squadron of the Royal Engineers, seventeen men named Smith.

17

On behalf of the Guests

My Mayor, Ladies and Gentlemen,

I'm honoured that you should have included me amongst your guests on this distinguished occasion and that you should also have charged me with the task of replying on behalf of my fellow guests to the toast, which has been proposed in his usual comprehensive and familiar way by our good friend, Alderman Rufflebotham.

We enjoyed the tour of the worthy Alderman's mind even if, for those who are not completely au fait with the current difficulties in the Town Clerk's office, the tour may appear to have been conducted in gathering darkness. We are all sorry, of course, that the Town Clerk can't be with us here this evening, but I think, on the whole, that he was wise to lie low until this wretched inquiry is over. You, more than any of us, Mr. Mayor, know how niggly these fellows from the CID can be.

There was no need, of course, for Alderman Rufflebotham to have apologised for going on so long, even though he obviously didn't mean us to take him too seriously. After all, the principal purpose of oratory (particularly if you are seventh on the toast list) is to stop other people from talking, and you were wise to make it clear that we had to be out of our lovely old drill hall by half past eleven, otherwise we might get you into trouble with the district auditor. We know all too well that his long experience makes him fussy about councillors claiming expenses for dining at another councillor's expense. I suppose, therefore, that our

104

toastmaster left early so that he could let your chauffeur know how the programme was going. It was kind of the headwaiter to help him find the way out, though I am sure that, given time, he would have managed it well enough for himself.

I now come back to the proposer of this toast. I must, of course, spare the Alderman's blushes, but I'm sure he will understand if I say that he is one of those people of whom it takes all sorts to make a world. Harry Rufflebotham (I may call you Harry, mayn't I? You've been telling me to do so even before I became a local director of your bank) – Good old Harry is quite a wag. I mean, that splendid joke of his about the Jew, the nigger and the cripple with the cleft palate – well, we mustn't be too touchy, must we? And, after all, he did say "Stop me if you've heard this one" and, since none of us could think of how to stop him, whom have we to blame except ourselves?

Harry is also a thorough man – he does nothing by half-measures as we can judge by the length and breadth of the speech which some of us have just enjoyed. After all, no man in a hurry is really civilised, and if anybody talks long enough, he is eventually bound by the laws of statistical probabilities to say something sensible. This happened to Alderman Harry on, I think, at least one occasion tonight, and, "Well done, that man," say I.

Mr. Mayor, there is much else for which we, your guests, may be thankful whilst congratulating you, as we must, upon your election at last to the mayoral chair of this borough.

We thank you first for your rare hospitality. I'm sorry, of course, that the borough's catering department has been robbed, amongst other things, of its head cook. He is, I understand, on his way to Australia for reasons of health, though you did not make it clear to us whether it was your health or his. It was typical, however, of your expertise in political economy that you should have called upon the pupils of the municipal cookery school to fill the gap and try and display some of their skill this evening on our behalf.

And, my word, what an exhibition it was. Speaking for myself, I *like* tinned hake. So, I am sure, does the Chief Constable, and his clear but obviously well-intended comments before he left, stemmed, I suspect, from the fact that he had inadvertently torn his trousers on the pile of discarded hake tins he came across in the dark behind the stockroom door and not from his amusement at the menu's witty reference to *La Merluche farcie au façon du Maire*. Well done, those pupils, too. They were prudent, I feel, in their compromise about the soup. I say this because some people are uneasy about averages – if a man has one foot in a refrigerator and the other on a red hot stove, then the statisticians maintain that, on an average, that man can be said to be comfortable. So be it, but whilst some like their *consommé en gelée*, others relish a red hot mulligatawny. You cannot, however, please all the people all the time and how diplomatic, therefore, of your budding young Escoffiers to serve us a soup that was tactfully cool.

A word of praise now, if I may, for your musical entertainment. A conservative like myself does not welcome the task of recognising all the noisy new tunes of the day. Mr. Mayor, the conductor of your municipal silver prize band is my friend! Long may he beguile us with his suave arrangements of *The Student Prince* and *In a Monastery Garden*, and long and lustrous may be the career of Miss Bertha Bellows, our blooming soprano soloist this evening. To attack in one programme the bell song from *Lakme, Lo, hear the gentle lark*, and the love motif from *Tristan and Isolde*, demands a courage that took our, and occasionally Miss Bellows' breath away. Though perfect or, indeed, near perfect pitch is not vouchsafed to everyone, we were amazed by her performance and I hope that someone will explain to her that it was only because the last bus for Runcorn leaves at 11.22 that those members of the Press who were still with us had to leave during her fourth encore and a little less quietly than usual. I am certain, however, that it will fall to our luck to hear Miss Bellows again.

I rejoice also, Mr. Mayor, that your customary last-minute readjustment of the seating plan gave me the honour of sitting next to your charming Mayoress. I'm a family man myself and I feel that as a result of all she had, in such refreshing detail, to tell me, I now know more about your own family than you do. Your Uncle Eric must be a scream, and I can't wait to see the twins. I'm sorry, of course, that owing presumably to a clerical oversight, you weren't able to invite my own wife to your repast tonight, but she, from long experience, will know exactly what she has missed.

Thank you also for reviving the long discarded ceremony of taking wine with your guests. The human race, to which so many members of the borough council belong, must be forgiven a little conceit. To stand up and be recognised in public is, for those who are still able to do so, an honour. We recognise your colleagues with acclaim and we shall also now welcome our greater ability to recognise them in good time when we see them coming towards us in the town.

The microphone, alas, is taking a night off but I think I understood the proposer of this toast to draw some financial lessons from the past in as much as they reflect upon our borough at the present. Assuming that Adam Smith, Ricardo, Keynes and Harold Wincott are all wrong, then Alderman Rufflebotham may well indeed be right. He tells us that the borough's fortunes are better this year than they were in the year gone by. This news may unfortunately not carry quite so much weight as seems to be the case at first blush. Harry puts me to mind of a report on a boy (whom I should like to have known) which hangs on the door of the prefect's study at my old school. It reads, if memory serves me right, as follows:

"This boy lies, steals and does not wash. That he has succeeded in seducing the under-matron, the gardener's wife and the captain of the school boxing team would not have mattered so much had not all three of these bizarre manifestations occurred within the same week. In this boy, sloth and corruption are combined in repellent harmony. But he has done much better than last term."

The imagination boggles (and I do not have a particularly boggly imagination) at what went on last term, so we think we understand what the speaker may mean when he says that the council has had a better year than last.

It was also perhaps just as well that in the course of his wide-ranging speech, Alderman Rufflebotham was painting on such a broad canvas that he was unable to include any reference to us, your guests and the subject of his toast. Nevertheless, we are grateful to him for everything he did say. Above all, we have one thing for which to thank him, and that is, of course, that he has shortened the winter for us.

18
Tails of Long Ago

I came across a photo the other day of King Edward VII at Baden Baden. He was surrounded by a coterie of friends, all encased in an impressive armoury of clothes. They sported thick serge suits, waistcoats, stiff shirts and stiffer collars, cravats and pins, watch chains, white insets, spats, and much other sartorial hors d'oeuvres. What they wore underneath beggars, as they say, description.

I gathered from the script alongside that most of these gentlemen normally looked after (in the expression of the day) some charming little thing. She either had a cosy nest in Maida Vale, or the Lessingstrasse, or the Rue Ste. Honoré. We know, of course, all about the ritual of the Cinq à Sept, and we remember how Mrs. Patrick Campbell yearned for the peace and quiet of the marriage bed after the hurly-burly of the chaise longue. I am now beginning to realise what she meant, but I still don't see how it was possible for those portly gentlemen at Baden Baden to have divested themselves of an appropriate quota of clothes, climbed into them again, and still coped with the job in hand within the statutory two hours' limit.

Until recently men's clothes, in my opinion, have been too heavy, too hot, and too complicated. England and Englishmen were at their best in the 1780's, and I should love to have strolled up St. James's Street with Beau Brummell at my side, and I don't doubt that I would have looked a dream. I wonder, though, how I should have liked to wear trousers in which I couldn't sit down, or whether I should have had the patience to tie a dozen cravats before perfection was obtained.

I hesitate to mention this, but personal hygiene must also have presented some problems. Dr. Johnson, as we know, was not over-fond of clean linen, and Fanny Burney, although she loved him dearly, preferred to sit opposite rather than next to him. What with greasy wigs and heavy fustian coats, all enclosing far too much port wine, I'm afraid that the members of the Club couldn't have radiated much sweetness after a particularly heavy session.

The same applies to the Elizabethans. I should have fancied myself in brocaded jackets, frills and furbelows, sword and plumed hat (whence panache, the splendid French word for a plume) but the whole *mise en scène* must have been as uncomfortable as it was insanitary. The Queen, we know, took a bath once a year whether she needed it or not. But what of your neighbours as you feasted off broiled swan, and roasted conies? You would certainly have needed that small bouquet of flowers!

Incidentally, the Elizabethans usually wore their hats at supper. The last man I saw behatted at the table was Lord Brabazon of Tara in the Coffee Room at the Carlton Club. And it was not so long ago that he and other Members of Parliament wore hats in the House of Commons. This was not just a foible; the purpose was to keep the glare from the glass roof out of their eyes. One Member, at the conclusion of an emotional speech, sat down upon his top hat. Mr. T. P. O'Conner, M.P., said it was lucky that the Hon. Gentleman's head wasn't in his hat at the time.

I haven't myself got a hat – at least, not a really respectable one. I only realised this when my oculist told me the other day not to wear dark glasses which weaken the eyes, but to wear a broad-brimmed hat which wards off the sun's rays more effectively. The only decent hat I could find was my coronet. This, of course, has no brim, and in any case it might appear slightly outré at Marrakesh, or on the beach at Napoule-sur-mer.

People still wear top hats at Ascot, and also, if they are Americans, when presenting their diplomatic credentials to the Queen. I thought that the U.S. Ambassador looked splendid as he set off for the Palace the other day in his top hat. But then he's a splendid looking chap in the first place. He was also wearing full evening dress, and, frankly, top hat, white tie and tails do look a little odd at 11 o'clock in the morning. Who ought to have been standing next to him? Well, Ginger Rogers, of course. But, no, it was the Marshal of the Diplomatic Corps wearing the full fig of a modern Major-General, complete with long, dark-blue dressing-gown and peering anxiously through a miasma of wind-blown, off-white plumes.

It's difficult to know where uniform ends and fancy dress begins. How do you distinguish between dignity and impudence? When I was at the Bar I remember conducting a case before Mr. Justice Hallett, never the quietest of judges. One defence witness was a teenaged gentleman with frizzy hair, and wearing jeans, below a T-shirt proclaiming that he Loved Lucy. Not unnaturally he was sent out of court with a flea in his ear. He complained to me about this outside. "Silly old git," he said, "what's he picking on me for? Look at 'im. Long red woolly nightie, dancing pumps, a nappie round his neck, and a soppy little periwig on 'is bonce." I must confess that I felt the lad had a point, but he remained unconsoled even when I told him that the highest court in the land, the House of Lords, adjudicates not in scarlet and ermine but in old and rather crumpled lounge suits.

Men are peacocks at heart. We feel that a different dress adds authority, and this, together with our innate love of ceremony, is why we have clung to our mayoral and aldermanic robes, our wigs and gowns, our mess kit, our toppers and our tails. Nevertheless, egalitarian comfort is creeping in. The Privy Councillor's uniform has gone: the frock coat, that most elegant of garments, has vanished. I believe Mr. Julian Amery is its last upholder. If Lady Butler's picture is to be believed, the

111

charge of the Black Watch with the Royal Scots Greys at Waterloo, all wearing thick scarlet serge and pipeclay, must have been a grand sight, but what with the French and the heat, conditions couldn't have been all that comfy. Not that our own battledress of 1939-45 was much better. It was smelly and scratchy – it was hot in summer, and gave you lumbago in winter. If you had to lie down in a hurry to avoid bits of metal passing overhead, your buttons flew off in all directions. And nobody is better than the Army at designing a hat which is guaranteed to give your eyes no protection from the sun, your neck none from the rain, and which, to coin a phrase, will fall off at the drop of a hat.

I am a nostalgic man myself, but we must not confuse nostalgia with discomfort. Nothing helps the good old days better than a bad old memory. I'm all for capes and codpieces, doublets and hose. But I'm also a man for comfort, and must confess that I also like sport shirts and espadrilles. Women, we know, do not dress to please themselves or their husbands. They dress to annoy other women. But we all have to be practical. The skirt line shoots up in the spring, and drops down in the winter. If skirt fashions did not move frequently, skirt-makers would go bankrupt. This theory is called built-in obsolescence, and it also applies to nylons and electric-light bulbs.

The theory applies less to men. I used to be a director of Burberrys. Our standard product was the straight, plain Burberry raincoat. Every time we tried to modernise the design there was an outcry. No opportunities for built-in obsolescence there. I remember one old boy coming in to the shop carrying a rather tattered, but still useful Burberry, over his arm. His grand-children had apparently told him it was over the hill. He must have a new one, and they would pay. Exactly the same design, please. When had he bought the old one? we asked. His father, he told us, had given it to him when he went off to the Boer War, with the Post Office Rifles. That was in the autumn of 1899.

We men may indeed be peacocks, but at least we are conservative peacocks.

19
Order! order!

"Of course, we must have order in the conduct of our public affairs," said Lord Melbourne, "but, for God's sake, not too much." Lord Melbourne was, as usual, right.

I feel sure, however, that he would have frowned at the readiness of modern MPs to pick up the mace and wave it about. That would have offended his sense of elegance and his dislike of publicity. Lord Simonds, a formidable Lord Chancellor of the sixties, held the mace in similar respect. When a newly joined peer crossed the floor of the House between the Woolsack and the table (a strictly forbidden trespass) the Lord Chancellor summoned him at once. "Never do that again, I beg of you," he said sternly; "I don't mind at all but the mace simply hates it."

Both in and out of Parliament, here and in other countries too, one's views about order naturally change with the times.

Would Lord Melbourne approve of the BBC's daily broadcast of affairs in Parliament? Come to think of it, do I? Too often the House of Commons is made to sound like a noisy kindergarten and the House of Lords seems to be manned exclusively by P. G. Wodehouse's pottier peers. Neither is a fair reflection of what actually happens, but it is unfortunately evidence of how difficult it is to edit a Parliamentary programme fairly, and without detracting from the dignity of the proceedings.

And if you think ill of the *yah boo, sucks* you've another sort of repartee which comes so much to the fore during question time in the Commons, just imagine what such broadcasts would have sounded like in the days when the Irish members regularly brought the debates to an uproarious standstill? And how would Charles I's row with Speaker Lenthall over the five members have sounded on a seventeenth century news broadcast?

Another difficulty is that disorder does not always occur when you most expect it, and very often a watchful if controversial TV camera comes in handier than a microphone. A lady who disapproved last year of what was going on in the Italian Parliament, stood up in the gallery and started to take all her clothes off by way of protest. That would have looked well on News at Ten. I wish, too, that the camera had been able to record the occasion when Manny Shinwell, understandably annoyed by some aspersions cast upon his upbringing by a certain Commander Strickland, crossed the floor of the House and fetched the gallant Commander a sharp clip over the ear. The Speaker, of course, had to order Mr. Shinwell out of the House, but his departure was watched with some sympathy.

Our attitude to straightforward verbal abuse has also changed considerably. We have noted with regret that the cut and thrust of debate in the Commons often comes over on the radio as unedifying farmyard uproar. Most of the insults that are handed out today seem far removed from the delicacy of Richard Brimsley Sheridan's "Mr. Speaker, Sir. I said that the Honourable Gentleman was a liar it is true and I am sorry for it." He went on to add that the Honourable Member could put the punctuation marks where he pleased.

Erskine May, the Politician's Bible, sets out a long list of the words you may not use in debate. You may not, for instance, address a colleague in either house as a slubberdegullion or a red-necked rustiguts, both of which have been tried in their time. In the Irish Parliament you won't get away with slubberdegullion either, but red-necked rustiguts appears to be quite in order.

There was neither an Erskine May and only occasionally a Speaker in the time of Henry VIII and since Martin Luther was, in addition, a Member of neither House, he could with relative impunity call the Monarch a pig, an ass, a dunghill, the spawn of an adder, a basilisk, a lying buffoon and a mad fool with a frothy mouth. All the same, I should have thought that, knowing Henry VIII, Luther was asking for trouble in a big way.

With care, however, you can be quite rude in Parliament without in any way transgressing the rules of order. I like Sir Harold Wilson's suave observation during Harold Macmillan's premiership that, whenever the Prime Minister returned from abroad, Rab Butler would go to the airport and grip him warmly by the throat. And I wish Hansard had recorded of whom it was that T. P. O'Connor said "The Hon. Gentleman disagrees. I can hear him shaking his head."

In the House of Lords slightly different rules prevail. This is not due to any senatorial hoity-toitiness. The reason we have to go about our business with circumspection is that we have no Speaker to call us to order if we kick over the traces. The House is its own arbiter of what few rules it does accept and the Lord Chancellor, unlike Mr. Speaker, has no disciplinary authority. Indeed, being himself a Member of the Government, he can from time to time find himself both the recipient and the begetter of barbed words. Just barbed; not, of course, disorderly.

Take the case of Lord Jowett. He was a good Lord Chancellor, but by no stretch of the imagination could he be called a popular one. The speed and eagerness with which he offered to turn his coat distressed his friends who were neither a numerous nor a sensitive body at the best of times.

When the date of the 1951 General Election was made known there was jubilation in the Tory ranks wherein victory could be scented. That was all well and good, said Lord Jowett, but would we kindly spare a thought for the poor old Lord Chancellor. Not only did he run the risk of losing his seat on the Woolsack, of which he was justly proud (indeed, indeed), but he and his wife would have to quit their comfortable flat in the House of Lords and start house-hunting which, at their age, was an unwelcome prospect. (Rhubarb! Rhubarb!) From the Tory back-benches came a blandly helpful suggestion. Had the Lord Chancellor thought of enquiring whether there was any accommodation available in the Vicarage of Bray? Lord Jowett was not amused.

Nor was Lord Hastings amused by a brush he experienced with the Whips during the Committee Stage of the Steel Bill. This set-to occurred in the Prince's Chamber which is technically outside the House itself and where the rules of order are accordingly even more lenient than within. Lord Onslow was the Whip on duty, stationed by the door to prevent peers slinking home when their presence was needed in the lobbies. This was just what Lord Hastings was clearly minded to do. "You can't go home now, Lord Hastings," said Lord Onslow. "Who said so?" asked Lord Hastings fiercely. (He was a very fierce man at the best of times which this, clearly, was not.) "The Chief Whip says so," replied Arthur Onslow. "B . . . the Chief Whip," said Lord Hastings, even more fiercely. Now this was not only a very disorderly approach, it might also have involved a potential breach of privilege. Arthur Onslow was duly shocked, but before he could gather his wits, Lord Hastings seized him by the lapels of his jacket and glared into his face. "And furthermore, Onslow," he said quietly, "despite the very warm and real affection in which I always held your dear father, b . . you too." And off he went.

The House of Lords is seldom disorderly in a physical sense – I mean no face-slapping or mace-waving or similar goings-on. There was, however, one disturbing occasion when Lord Airlie brought a gin-trap into the House and put it on the floor to illustrate a point he was making in a speech about cruelty to animals. (We're very keen on animals in the House of Lords. You'll get just as long a list of speakers in a debate on the preservation of ospreys as you will on Defence or Economics.) Well, you're not really allowed to bring anything into the House, not even a brief-case, let alone a gin-trap. One of the Hansard reporters, coming in to take up his place, failed to notice the trap, trod on it and went about limping for weeks.

We don't, however, have so many things thrown at us as they do in the Commons. This is very disorderly conduct indeed and it is unfortunately becoming more common. In the recent past, the Commons have been bombarded from the galleries with stink bombs, bags of horse-dung, pots of paint and, of course, the usual confetti-like shower of leaflets.

Somebody once threw a bowler-hat at my father when he was speaking at the despatch-box on the Currency and Bank Notes Bill. The missile was actually intended for Sir Archie Southby who was sitting on the bench behind, and it was aimed at him by a disgruntled constituent who apparently disapproved of the way in which his Member was handling some problems connected with his pension. Everybody thought it was a bomb and ducked. My father, however, carried on as if nothing was amiss and was much praised for his coolness. He confessed afterwards that being very short-sighted, he had not noticed that anything was happening at all.

I am glad to say that I myself have never once in nearly forty years' membership been involved in any disorderly conduct. At least, not of my own making. I do, however, remember an awkward moment involving that charming actress, the late Vivien Leigh. She had come to listen to a debate (which I was to wind up on behalf of the Government) concerning the proposed demolition of the St. James's Theatre. She was sitting in Black Rod's guest box, and just before I got up to speak, she rose to her feet and launched into an impassioned oration. Now this, of course, was horribly out of order so Black Rod (Sir Brian Horrocks) leant forward and whispered loudly "You'll have to go now." Miss Leigh apparently misheard him and thought he had said "You have a go now" which is not quite the same thing; but before she could get her second wind, the door-keepers had bustled her out.

Shaken, I started off on my own speech only to be interrupted by the impish Lord Stansgate (father to Anthony Wedgwood Benn). He reproved me for ignoring the usual courtesies. I had, he said, forgotten to congratulate the lady on her maiden speech.

I resisted the temptation and ploughed on but, I am afraid, with my sang a little less froid than I hope is usual.

Hansard recorded the whole disorderly episode with the one word "Interruption".

20
Tycoonery

To the pedant, tycoon means *tai kun*, the Japanese warlord of mediaeval times. To you and me it means Mr. Max Joseph, Sir Isaac Wolfson, and the hall-porter at the Savoy.

Not all tycoons, of course, are cast in such a stately mould. There was once a company whose chairman evinced, as they say, a very low profile. It was practically horizontal. But his staff were fond of the old buffer, so, in order to help him, they pinned a note inside the balance sheet amongst his agenda papers. "The credit side," it read, "is the one nearest the window."

I hope this story is legendary, but I'm not quite so sure. As recently as 1960 a Government Report described traditional British business management as being "mixed in concrete". Hoping that tycoonery can be taught they set up the London Graduate School of Business Studies, which now regards itself as the Oxbridge of British business schools. I don't know whether it is more successful than other British schools at turning out tycoons, but its premises in the Nash terraces of Regent's Park are certainly the prettiest.

The doyen of all tycoon teaching is, of course, the Harvard Business School in the USA. Any similarity between the HBS and a monastery is, of course, fully intended. The school's curriculum talks of "total immersion in an academic atmosphere with minimum outside attractions." They take their business very much before their pleasure, and I know what I'm talking about because I once had the terrifying experience of lecturing at Harvard. My audience heard me with the rapt attention of all American audiences, though so many earnest young Americans look like so many other earnest young Americans that it is not easy to tell whether they have genuinely wrapped their attention or are merely thinking about sex or their prospects of promotion. Their first question, however, restored my morale. "Is it really true," one Ivy Leaguer asked, "that you can still buy a baby crocodile at Harrods?"

Although I am happy to learn that there are now 41 business schools in Britain, I still wonder whether you can really teach tycoonery at all. So does Sir Arnold Weinstock, the articulate managing director of GEC. "Business," he says, "is about relationships with people, including differences in culture and background. Management is largely judgement and I don't see how you can teach judgement."

To which, he might have added, you can't teach luck or chutzpah either, both of which play a larger part in business success than some tycoons are prepared to admit.

Brains, of course, help too. Sir Isaac Wolfson's father, Solomon Wolfson, was never a businessman; he was a quiet scholar, and when some visitors began to discuss monetary matters with him, he threw up his hands in dismay. "Go to my son, Isaac," he said, "He's the financial genius around here. Brilliant! Fantastic!" "And how old is this paragon?" they asked. "Nine," said Solomon Wolfson, with pride.

You are not to think, however, that I would hear ill spoken of the mechanics of tycoonery. I am a vigorous supporter of the discounted cash-flow, though I suspect that Nuffield and Duveen got along well enough without it. It is certainly more than useful to be able to read a balance sheet, if only to keep your accountant in his proper place. John Pierpont Morgan, not a lovely man at the best of times, taught himself to read a balance sheet upside down, and this must have come in handy when he was seeking to do business with a competitor across his desk. I yield to no man in my respect for critical path analysis, but I also think that Mr. Umberto Agnelli, of Fiat, has a point when he says that management is not the exact science that some HBS professors would have us believe. Indeed, I have much sympathy with Mr. Peter Cohen, of the HBS itself, who actually goes so far as to declare that the maximization of long-range profits is not why God hath created the Earth. My word! Talk about cats and pigeons!

I think well, too, of the views of Mr. Akio Morita, President of Sony of Japan, "I believe," he argues, "that the best initial training is hard-knock practical experience. Then we should go back to school to learn, like going to a gym to flex one's muscles."

This is interesting, coming from a Jap. The Americans take a man on for results. The Japs take a man on for life. And both seem to think that the British take a man on because he's the Chairman's nephew. I am a staunch believer in the hereditary system, and accordingly I call in evidence Sir Leonard Wolfson, Mr. Bobby Butlin, Sir Max Aitken, and Mr. Anthony Tuke. Tycoonery can be inherited as well as taught. And if the Chairman's nephew is to join the Board you can be pretty sure, in these rough days, that the Chairman is not going to risk his reputation by importing an illiterate oaf, and, after all, he knows the lad better than the rest of his colleagues.

I'm also a great believer in non-executive tycoonery. The foreigners all laugh at us for putting so many retired generals and ambassadors onto the Boards of our insurance companies and our banks. What, they ask, can they know about ergonomics or charter-parties? Little enough, in all conscience, but at least they may know enough about the handling of human beings to prevent the Chairman from committing an injustice, or the professional management from losing their heads. (Not always, of course, as I myself once discovered to my cost when the Arabs forced me off the Norwich Union board.)

Not everybody loves a tycoon. The asset-strippers,

the bond-washers and the property whizz-kids are now examined with an increasingly critical eye. Mr. Tiny Rowland did well enough for his Lonrho shareholders, but there were other important principles involved. Mr. Peter Cohen, again, has pointed out that today's emphasis on competition, on winning, on making a fast buck is a case study of individualism gone mad. Mr. Heath said much the same thing, but not quite so politely. In some respects the City has unfortunately become a four-letter word. But the face of capitalism is sometimes unacceptable to different people for different reasons. When the Seamen's Union said they would like to have a representative on the Board of Cunard, Cunard said Yes, certainly, provided Cunard could have a representative on the Council of the Seamen's Union. And answer came there none.

There are, of course, some tricks of tycoonery which cannot be picked up either at Harvard or in Regent's Park. Lord Nuffield once wanted to join a certain Golf Club, but some of the members thought otherwise and black-balled him. So he bought the whole Club, threw out the black-ballers, and put his supporters onto the committee.

I bet Lord Nuffield didn't need anybody to teach him that piece of tycoonery.

21
My future Wives

My Uncle George was happily married to Auntie Maud for nearly fifty-three years. Seeing that he used to smoke a strong Burma cheroot in bed every night and then relight it again in the morning I think this reflects well on the patience and forbearance of my Aunt. Indeed, on the occasion of their golden wedding, I ventured to ask her if, in the course of what must have been fifty exacting years, she had ever contemplated divorcing the old buzzard. She thought this over carefully and then replied, "Divorce? No, never; of course not. Murder, yes, several times. But never divorce."

When I add that he used to refer to her in public as "My first wife" in order, as he explained, to keep her on her toes, you will be able to assess the measure of her forbearance.

The fact that my Uncle George's father had been shot in the ear by his mistress in a tram in Valparaiso must have warned her (if she had any belief in the laws of genetics) that her married life was unlikely to be humdrum; and it wasn't. It was nevertheless happy, very happy, and if you'd asked my Uncle George to give his opinion about *his* next wife, you'd have got the rough edge of the most abrasive tongue in the county of Norfolk.

I only mention this in order to establish the fact that any speculations about my own next wife are purely hypothetical and are not to be taken as criticism of the situation presently obtaining in our corner of Chelsea.

When a man marries for the first time he is venturing into the dark. When he marries for the second time, he remembers where he stubbed his toe. I am sure, therefore, that I wouldn't want just another wife. One wife alone could not, in the future, fulfil all my requirements.

I'd want about twelve wives to do the job properly and what's wrong with polygamy anyhow? Wouldn't a move in that direction be in keeping with the times?

The Gay Brigade have at long last got their way with homosexuality. Parliament has set the seal of its approval on sexual relations between consenting male adults and this in spite of the fact that the man in the street seems dead against it and has been for a thousand years. Not, of course, that the opinion of the man in the street matters any longer at Westminster.

Abortion is now apparently in and the House of Lords was thought to be squeamish for having given voice to such old-fashioned disquiet. Pot and pop go hand in hand and in next to no time it'll be hurrah for incest. So what, I ask, is wrong with a little polygamy?

It's already practised with genteel approval in many of the African communities that now share with us the burdens of civilisation. It is also well thought of in Malaya and Polynesia and, in a way, it is also popular in the United States of America, though under slightly different rules. Americans don't have all their wives at the same time. The French have lots of mistresses but only one wife because they don't believe in divorce. The Americans think well of divorce but that's because their mistresses insist on becoming their wives, if not for very long. Since America is a matriarchy and the girls have all the money, this can be important. American gentlemen accordingly accept the implications of alimony more calmly than the British. For my part it has always seemed that paying alimony is like buying carrots for a dead donkey.

Signing on twelve wives will, of course, permit of some margin of error. I was always a devoted admirer of Miss Marilyn Monroe. What, when drunk, one saw in other women, one saw in Marilyn Monroe when sober. She could hardly, however, have been regarded as the perfectly domesticated wife, the sort who can always find in a bottom drawer the sock that isn't there.

In each of my twelve wives, therefore, I shall look for one of the assets that go to make up the dodecahedronal woman who, mercifully does not exist. If she did, the Prime Minister, not himself wishing to vacate 10 Downing Street, would presumably appoint her to the Woolsack tomorrow. The right of a woman to become Lord Chancellor has now been soundly established as has also her right to train racehorses. A woman can not yet, however, become a member of the London Stock Exchange nor, I think, Archbishop of Canterbury. Much more important, a woman cannot propose marriage. A proposal of marriage still has to come from the man and the woman still has to make it look as if that was the way it happened. Too many women, in retaliation, regard a marriage licence as a licence to drive a man, and that's one of the reasons why I am in favour of polygamy. By that process you can divide and, given a modicum of luck, you can also rule.

At least fifty per cent of my team must have both beauty and charm (The beauties are the ones that I notice and the charmers the ones that notice me.) I shall also, of course, want an expert pianist, a blue riband cook, a petit-pointiste of genius, a tolerably competent political dialectician and a girl who can mend a fuse.

A few level heads will be needed, too. We're an unreasonable lot, we husbands. We point out rudely that mother nature decorated the humming-bird, the kingfisher and the dragon-fly in vivid and dazzling hues, but the rhinoceros, the hippopotamus and the elephant are all turned out in a plain and decent grey. We accordingly beg our wives not to overdo it. Neat, we suggest, but not gaudy. We applaud when they accompany us to a rout or soirée in quiet and sober attire. We then spend the evening gawping goggle-eyed at some little piece of nonsense clad in three bits of eau-de-nil Elastoplast and wearing an Israeli melon on her head.

We must therefore, I repeat, have some sobersides in

126

our team. I accept that a woman who will listen to reason is probably thinking of something else but I shall want at least one wife who will take her time, who will make up her mind slowly and whose final decision will not necessarily be the one she will eventually take. I admire a woman who can suffer in silence though I realise she may have a lot to say later on. If she is inquisitive, she must be intelligently inquisitive; in other words, she must learn to ask the sort of questions I can answer.

And all twelve of them have got to be healthy. This, I realise, is an uncouth request and I'm ashamed of it but I simply cannot put up with other people's ailments. If I myself am smitten with the gout or toothache or Webster's disease or what have you, then all my twelve wives must display sympathy and understanding. For my part, I shall not be able to tolerate any one of them suffering from so much as a chilblain. Sultan Abdul the Damned had about two hundred and thirty-four wives (etc) but so sensitive was he to infirmity that it took him less than twenty minutes to discover if any one of them was suffering from lumbago. Some people can tell the moment a cat or a baronet enters the room. Sufferers from ill-health have the same effect on me. Another bee in my bonnet and one of which I am not particularly proud.

I realise, of course, that polygamy is a counsel of perfection. Monogamy is more chancy. You marry one woman in particular and the next morning you wake up to discover you have married somebody else. And you will soon learn from her own lips the sort of man she would have preferred to marry. Not, of course, that a man should ever express a counter-opinion on such a delicate matter as this. A woman who is sensible enough to ask her husband's advice is seldom stupid enough to take it.

I have visited Malaya on several occasions and Polynesia once. I forgot, I'm afraid, to raise the question of polygamy. I discussed, at length, such burning issues as the future of containerisation in the Pacific freight trade and even, if I remember aright, the relevance of pot in swinging Wolverhampton, but not, alas, the niceties of polygamy as they affect the run-of-the-mill Briton who might be thinking of taking a second wife.

The men I know who get on well with women are usually those who know how to get on without them. I should like, in this context, to have consulted the Texan millionaire whose will was recently challenged by his next-of-kin in the probate court of Dallas. The will, which was correctly signed and witnessed, consisted of only one sentence. "Give Mabel the works." Mabel got the works and bully for Mabel. Her gentleman evidently knew when he was well off. If he had been given the chance, he would obviously have married Mabel again, assuming that he had actually married her in the first place.

Some people tut-tut when a widower remarries quickly. I don't. I think it's a great compliment to his first wife for having made him realise that two is company and widowerhood is none.

There's a lot to be said for polygamy, but there's more to be said for Mabel. And what's more, with Mabel, you don't get twelve mothers-in-law.

22
If only

If only Mr. Moyses Stevens, the florist, hadn't suffered a momentary lapse of memory, my Uncle Harry wouldn't have been able to leave me a pipe of the Cockburn 1912 in his Will. What happened was this.

Uncle Harry was a great man for sending people flowers. People (particularly young female people) liked this, and they also liked the fact that his bouquet was always accompanied by a little card carrying an appropriate message, written in his own fair hand. No typed cards or florists' handwriting for Uncle Harry! What people didn't know was that he kept an assorted stock of pre-written cards with Mr. Moyses Stevens. One, for instance, said simply "Hurrah!" This did well enough for births, marriages, engagements, and the advent of unexpected legacies, whilst another, saying, "I am so *deeply* distressed" came in handy for deaths, divorces, and legacies that failed.

One evening, Uncle Harry was dining with the parents of a little red-headed piece named Maisie, upon whom he had designs. Unfortunately, whilst waving an arm to emphasise a nicely worded point, he inadvertently bowled a sauce-boat into the lap of Maisie's mother. His hostess was a mite disenchanted about this, so next morning Uncle Harry ordered a handsome bouquet to be dispatched. Unfortunately, Mr. Moyses Stevens, instead of pinning on the deeply distressed card, accidentally sent the one which read, "What a wonderful evening! When can we do it again?" Poor Uncle was immediately banished from copper-nob's company, and what might have turned into a lasting romance was brought to a peremptory halt. Uncle Harry, as a matter of fact, never married at all, and eventually spent what spare shillings he could muster in collecting Piranesi prints and vintage port, and this, if only Mr. Stevens had been more thoughtful, might never have come my way.

With the possible exception of "Time, gentlemen, please," I regard the words "What might have been" as the saddest in the English language. They probably sound nearly as dispiriting in Urdu, Swahili, and Malay, and I know for certain that they do in German. When I was a student at Bonn University there used to hang in the English library a framed quotation from the poet Heine with a helpful translation underneath, "Opportunity may only knock at your door once in a lifetime. Grasp it: it may never return." Some savant had crossed out the word "lifetime" and substituted "nightdress" – but the sentiment remained a noble one.

Noble, but debatable. Some missed opportunities may eventually prove to be blessings in disguise. Uncle Harry used to tell me that one of the minor pleasures of middle age was looking back at the girls he hadn't married. And who knows whether Maisie might not have turned out a real vixen, and nagged the poor old boy into an early grave? We tend to put all our mistakes into a heap and call them our misfortunes. I suspect that "what might have been" might as often as not accrue to our distress. Do we not only remember the lost opportunities from which we might have profited, and conveniently forget the ones that would inevitably have landed us in the mud? That's the trouble with *ifonliness*.

If only I'd marked Leeds United to win at home last Saturday I might well be dining off *pâté de foie gras* to the sound of trumpets for the rest of my life. If only I'd bought Better Mousetraps instead of switching into IOS I might now be nuzzling some blonde on the deck of my yacht at Antibes. That's all very well, but you forget that if you hadn't marked Norwich City to draw, and if you hadn't picked up Cunard when they were only eleven bob, you might well now be in the poor house.

Even the shrewd Israelis are not proof against this confusion of thought. They mutter, for instance, and shake their heads whenever the name of Moses is mentioned. If you ask them why this should be they reply, "Well, think. If only the old gentleman had turned right instead of left when he brought the Children of Israel out of the Wilderness, we might now have oil instead of all these confounded oranges."

Well, that's as may be; and whilst we are out in Mesopotamia, what about the Garden of Eden? If only Eve had done what she was told, and left that wretched apple untasted, we might all be better situated than we are today. But you can't bet on it. I've always regarded poor Eve as a bit of a rattle-brain, and if the author of Genesis c.3 has got his facts right she was also very short of tact. So even if she had managed to pull herself together and send the serpent about his business, she would probably have dug another heffalump trap for herself in a couple of days, and done something equally chuckle-headed. Then we'd all be in the same old mess as before.

By and large, History comes down firmly against the wisdom of moaning about what might have been. If only, for instance, Guy Fawkes had actually succeeded in blowing up the House of Commons, do you really think we should have been saved from Oliver Cromwell? I doubt it. And if only Christopher Columbus had listened to his crew, and turned back when their courage failed them, would America have remained undiscovered for long? Of course not. In next to no time some other Nosey Parker would have cast off for Atlantis, or El Dorado, or whatever it was they were all looking for, only to bump eventually into Boston by mistake.

And now Lord Harvey of Tasburgh's Diplomatic Diaries have set the pundits by the ears. If only the General's Assassination putsch had not so narrowly failed and if only we had called Hitler's bluff at the time of Munich, could we not have prevented World War II? And has anybody explained what would have happened if only Hitler had declared war on Japan at the time of Pearl Harbour, and thus aligned himself with America? Would America have rejected Germany's advances? But the piece of history that really worries me is this. What would have happened if only Pontius Pilate had not changed his mind about Barabbas?

But all this is a little above our station. For us ordinary mortals, it's the pillow-biter by which we judge the importance of what might have been. You know, of course, what a pillow-biter is? You wake up in the middle of the night, and you break into a muck sweat as memories come flooding back of some ghastly brick that you once dropped, or some unpardonable solecism you long ago committed. So you bite your pillow in the agony of remorse. "If only I had not drunk so much at the Wotherspoon wedding, and thrown my arms so effusively around the Archdeacon's neck as my wife was anxiously wheeling me home, might I not now be Chairman of the Rural District Council?" "If only I had not put all those white mice in the Science Master's shirt drawer, might I not have won that splendid scholarship to Wolverhampton Tech.?"

My own worst pillow-biter was conceived in the officers' ward room of the SS *William H. Daniels* on 5 June 1944. We were at the time lying off Southend, waiting to proceed next day to the beaches of Normandy in the normal course of business. About seven hundred of us had been living for nearly a week in exhilarating discomfort on the open deck of this scruffy but hospitable little petrol coaster. Her officers were the soul of kindness, and they unselfishly let about forty of us eat in rotation in their miniscule Mess. As I waited my turn for a place at the table I was gazing out of the port-hole towards Southend, a view which we had been admiring for several days and of which we were by that time heartily sick. "Heavens above," I exclaimed in exasperation, "how much longer are we going to be kept hanging about here?" I was referring, of course, to Southend, but the poor little Chief Engineer, snatching a hurried meal of beans and bacon at his own table, obviously thought I was complaining about the length of time I had been kept waiting for luncheon. "I've been eating as fast as I can," he muttered, and left the room.

If only I had realised in time how horrifyingly I had been misunderstood. But it was too late. I never saw him again to apologise, and I still bite my pillow in recollection of this enormity. If only he reads this, I may be able to put the matter to rights; if only this catches his eye I shall invite him, by way of atonement, to help me polish off Uncle Harry's port.

23
A few light Snacks

When Boswell and Johnson were visiting the Isle of Mull, their hostess offered them cold sheep's head for breakfast. At the thought of this delicacy, even the Doctor's formidable gorge rose in revolt, and he waxed indignant about the incident in his *Journal*. So, more quietly, did Boswell in his.

Both works carried such detailed descriptions of what the two friends ate and drank that Mrs. Thrale brought it upon herself to reprove them. It was not nice, she told them firmly, for a gentleman to show so much care for his sustenance. Johnson replied sharply that if a man didn't care for his belly he would care for nothing.

I daren't think what Mrs. Thrale would have to say on this subject if she were alive today. There's more written now about food and drink than about anything else except sex and race relations. Pretty well every newspaper and magazine has its regular wine correspondent. Even our local paper in Gloucestershire has entered the lists. Last month's County wine-making contest, for instance, attracted serious attention. Winners in the home-made claret section were Mrs. X (fruity, well-rounded), Mrs. Y (fine colour and full-bodied), and Miss Z (slightly acid, but should improve if laid down).

In wider journalistic fields all tastes are catered for, from admirers of the 1924 Mouton Rothschild to devotees of Château Plonque. In *The Financial Times* Edmund Penning-Rowsell deploys an expertise in keeping with the rest of the paper. Andrew Graham has, alas, been forced by illness to leave *The Times*, where his scholarly and gentle notes are much missed. Pamela Vandyke Price has taken his place. She appears to enjoy controversy, but even so, she mustn't encourage us to drink whisky with oysters. Cyril Ray in *The Director* wanders entertainingly off the beaten track, particularly in Italy and Central Europe. He even finds nice things to say about Cyprus sherry, but he is not well-briefed about borage. In *Harpers & Queen* Humphrey Lyttleton is practical, critical and very funny. He rightly deserved to win a Glenfiddick Prize as the wine-and-food writer of the year. (But as I was one of the judges I am naturally biased.)

There are now dozens of expert wine writers to suit all tastes and every prejudice. A particular prejudice of my own is a distrust of over-decorative writing. Even the magisterial André Simon could not always resist temptation, and when he spoke rapturously of a full body, a delicate nose, and a prospect of well-developed ripeness, one might be forgiven for asking whether he was discussing Brigitte Bardot or the Vosne-Romanée, La Grande Rue, 1949.

James Thurber did much to sober us up when he offered a naïve little Burgundy, and hoped that we would be "amused by its presumption". And Stephen Potter, with tongue still further in cheek, spoke of "the imperial decay of his invalid port, its gracious withdrawal from perfection, keeping a hint of former majesty withal as it hovered between oblivion and the divine *untergang* of infinite recession". The circle of wine writers under the Chairmanship of Sir Trevor Lloyd-Hughes, K.B., M.A., rightly disapproves of such flourishes, but not, I suspect, without a wistful sigh of regret.

Making speeches about wine requires even more control than writing about it. I have been asked to do so only once, and I failed with ignominy. Together with Sir David Webster (the late Director-General of Covent Garden Opera) I was to be installed as a Commandeur du Tastevin in Burgundy. The ceremony began at 6.30

p.m., when 600 of us sat down to dinner in the caves of the Clos de Vougeot. Seven wines and five hours later, I was suddenly, and without warning, called upon to make a speech in French. Not only was I by then unable to utter a single word of French – I could say very little in English either. Indeed, I could hardly stagger to my feet.

It was just as well that we had taken the precaution of bringing our chauffeur with us. Unfortunately, however, he had forgotten the name of the hotel in Dijon where we lodged. So, at about two o'clock in the morning we were to be found circulating between the Toison d'Or, the Chapeau Rouge and the Central Hotel, where puzzled night porters were asked if they could lay any claim to the somnolent Commandeurs in the back.

To all those who write about wine, let alone speak about it, I raise my glass. Thanks to their work, many of us have acquired increasing knowledge and appreciation of one of the delights that distinguish the Barbarian from the civilised man. I envy their enthusiasm and expertise. I am glad, too, that they are now writing for the man of humble means and humbler cellar space, rather than just for the millionaire.

They have, of course, in this country, an advantage over their foreign brethren, because, with all respect to General Sir Guy Salisbury Jones, the doyen of British wine-growers, we grow no great wine here ourselves. Try asking for claret in Cologne, or Mosel in Marseilles, and you'll see the advantage this gives not only to the British wine-bibbler, but to his advisers, too. The British writer has a wider vineyard in which to range, and many more grapes from which to choose.

I was put in mind of this the other day when I was looking through my Guzzle Book. This is my own modest and rather disreputable contribution to the literature of wine and food. In it I've noted down over the years meals I have particularly enjoyed, and wines which I wished to remember. There is a number for the food, a letter for the wine, an asterisk for the ambience, and a nominal roll of the company present.

During a particularly uncomfortable period of the war, when my Regiment was replete with Spam and biscuits, some of us who had travelled together in happier times used to compose meals from memory, just to cheer ourselves up. I would start with the main course – say 27F (This had been enjoyed at M. Thulier's Oustau de Baumanière near Les Baux-de-Provence: a superb Gigot d'Agneau en Croûte helped down with a new Gigondas.) "Well," responded my Battery Captain, "we shall want something pretty light before that, shan't we? What about 18K?" "Agreed." (This was a brook trout lately swimming in its tank outside the Goldener Hirsch at Neuenahr, and escorted by a mouthful of Piesporter Michelsberg. Nice stuff.)

One item in the book which recently caught my eye had, however, slipped my memory. 117K. Against it I had put both a question and an exclamation mark. I rang up the particular friend with whom I had shared that luncheon.

"Donald," I said, "117K." "Of course," he replied. "The New Inn at Coln St. Aldwyns."

"But why the exclamation mark, and why the query? What was it about that lunch that both aroused our excitement and raised questions in our minds? Was it the Lafite '53, or the wonderful steak-and-kidney pudding, with mushroom sauce, tender spring greens and dear little new potatoes?"

"Don't be daft," my friend replied, "it was nothing to do with the meal at all. It was the waitress."

One day I may come across a man who has married a girl for her knowledge of claret. That'll be a turn-up for the book.

24
The City by Night

My mother once had a loin of pork lobbed into her lap as she was driving back from a dance to her home in the Charterhouse. This *must* have been an accident. The Smithfield meat porters knew her well by sight and this was hardly surprising because she was a very pretty girl and in those days there weren't many pretty girls living in the heart of the City. And, come to think of it, I don't suppose there can be many more living there today.

There are of course two cities of London. There's the City of the day – the Square Mile teeming with a financial expertise and an integrity that is the envy of all beholders but a city which can occasionally drop a few interesting bricks. Then comes the evening and the markets are hushed. The paper darts are garnered from the floor of the Stock Exchange and gnarled night watchmen begin to thump around Lloyds and the Baltic. The Bears, the Bulls, the Stags and a million other sharp-witted animals get their bowler-hatted heads down for the 6.21 to Rickmansworth.

After that you can see the City of the night and a very odd place it is, too. It's a City of lonely policemen, of cleaners, cats and fish-porters. It's a place of empty streets, deserted pubs and of sudden, suprisingly beautiful vistas. The spire of St. Bride's (the Madrigal in Stone) looks even more delicious at midnight against a full August moon than it does when you're stuck beneath it in a traffic block on your way to an urgent noon-time appointment. "Not to worry," said my taxi driver consolingly. "Defence of the Realm comes into all this. If the Russians landed tomorrow, I reckon hey'd get no further than Ludgate Hill."

So be it, but I find the City of the night more fascinating than the day. When my grandfather was resident physician to the Old Brothers of the Charterhouse, scarcely more than 10,000 people lived in the City. He worshipped in St. Bartholomew the Great, which was the only Norman church to resist both the Fire of 1666 and Hitler. In Victorian days, however, it was in a sad state of disrepair. The roof leaked, so the Rector, Sir Borrodaile Savory, had to hold up an umbrella whilst he was preaching, and his sermons were inclined to harp upon Noah, floods, and the waters of Babylon. The churchwardens eventually took the hint and sent for a tiler.

The City churches are fuller now than they were in my mother's day because they are open during the lunch hour for the benefit of a gratifyingly large number of City workers. But by night the City looks as desolate as it did fifty years ago, though my stockbroker tells me there's a restaurant which actually deploys belly dancers. Montagu Norman and my grandfather must be turning in their graves.

For some people the quiet can be overpowering. Between the wars Bombadier West in my regiment took a job as a caretaker with one of the City companies. He was a convivial fellow, born in Birmingham's Bull Ring and he liked noise. The utter silence of the City after dark got so much on his nerves that he eventually went mad. Bonkers. Right off his chump. They took him along to all the best chump doctors in Harley Street but to no avail. Then somebody had the bright idea of sending him back to stay with his Auntie May who earned her living as a cleaner at New Street Station in Birmingham. She lived in a small box over No. 7 platform and the racket was appalling, but it did the trick. In a few weeks the old boy was back in the City of London and as right as rain.

Incidentally, I believe the Lord Mayor is dining with another of the great City companies, the Worshipful

Company of Balloonblowers, this very evening, and the thought of this makes me revise my theory of the two Cities. There are, of course, actually three – day, night and this, the City of civic, gastronomic and oratoria twilight. A Lord Mayor of London has to make about 1,000 speeches a year, though some Lord Mayors have compromised by making the same speech 1,000 times. In the course of these endeavours the Lord Mayor will also have to eat in public about five hundred times and unless he has a stomach like the QE2's boilers this will probably damage him for life. If it doesn't, then having to listen to about 4,000 speeches from other people undoubtedly will.

But oddly enough, London is not all that full of dying Lord Mayors, ailing Aldermen and broken-down Masters of City Companies. This is a tribute to their own ambition and stamina as well as to the remarkable skill of Messrs. Ring & Brymer, the caterers who for about three hundred years have nourished City functions out of hay-boxes, billy cans and Aldershot ovens slung together in Cannon Street, since few of the City halls seem to have any kitchens.

It's easy of course to laugh at the pomp of the Lord Mayoralty and poke fun at the circumstance of civic fol-de-rol. I don't. Napoleon maintained that as long as he had enough red and blue silk ribbon, he would never lack brave generals.

All right. Too few Masters of the Worshipful Company of Balloonblowers have anything to do with balloons? They only got into the act because their wives liked the idea of knight-hood? Too few Lord Mayors come from the leading City institutions? Too many have only been ambitious estate agents commuting from Pinner who liked the idea of a baronetcy even though they now have to settle for a GCMG?

Possibly. But the City of London is governed more efficiently and more honestly than any other capital in the world. And by and large it's these Balloonblowers who do it and though their wives may from time to time give them a meaningful nudge, most of them really do have the interests of the City at heart and are proud of its history, lavish in their charity and jealous of the City's customs and traditions.

And talk about hospitable! To be entertained by the Lord Mayor of London is still a privilege which the visitor rightly covets, be he Duke or Dustman. I remember being bidden by my friend, Sir Cullum Welch, when he was Lord Mayor, to a party in honour of some visiting potentates from Polynesia. Sir Cullum, hospitable fellow that he is, did them proud – State Trumpeters, Daimler Hire, flood-lighting, Moët et Chandon, and a veritable cornucopia of civic oratory, spilling far into the night. Many of the guests spoke only a delightful pidgin English and in due course their comments in this tongue came back. "Much meat," they reported. "Wine him bubble. Bugle him tootle. Big fella Cullum, him quack, quack. Big fella ten time him quack, quack. Plenty candle, plenty ricksha. Him sleepy time juju."

And talking of juju, what about the City's politics? Conservative of course, but not always as conservative, as Central Office would like. The City used to be a separate constituency of its own but the Socialists put a stop to all that and made the City muck in with the neighbours down the road. The last City member was Sir Harold Webbe and I remember once taking a meeting for him when he lay sick of the palsy. It was a lunch-time meeting, of course. In the City politics die after dark, but at lunchtime they can be lively. My meeting was noisy by the City's refined standards, but when I had finished, the loudest heckler came up and to my astonishment told me that I had converted him. Furthermore, as a proof of his sincerity, he would like to join the Conservative Party. What was the smallest sum he would have to pay to join the Party? A shilling. He gave me a shilling and I gave him a receipt. I shook hands with him. The chairman shook hands with him. We were all photographed shaking hands with each other. I took him along to the "Green Man", hard by the Mansion House and bought him a double whisky. I gave him a brief resumé of our Party's manifesto and bought him another double whisky. I then rang up Harold Webbe and told him what had happened. "Good heavens," he said, "don't tell me that fellow's caught you, too. He must have had more double whiskies for a shilling than any other man in London."

A tribute to the financial enterprise of the City if not to its integrity. But that was at lunchtime. You couldn't get away with that sort of thing after dark. Neither the Lord Mayor, nor the Sheriffs, nor the Master, nor even the Wardens would put up with it for a moment. *Domine* (as the City's motto goes) *dirige nos*.

25
Name dropping

I'm proud to say that I now know quite a few Lieutenant-Generals and a fine body of men they are, too. But in June 1944 I knew hardly any, so when my Colonel told me that the Corps Commander was reported to be visiting our beaches in order to see what we were up to and would I kindly go and look after him, I naturally straightened myself out pretty smartly. Actually, there was a lull in the proceeding that morning and we weren't up to very much. We were humping petrol, washing our smalls, writing home to mother and taking the fuses out of those wretched Tellermines. I soon tracked our General down. He was watching a working party – Sgt. Jackson in charge – and Sgt. Jackson for his part was very intently watching our General. There was no saluting or anything like that; all very *Daily Mirror* and democratic. I was embarrassed. "What's the matter, Sergeant?" I asked in a loud stage whisper. "Have you never seen a Lieutenant-General before?" "Oh yes, sir, yes," he replied, "but that's the first one I've ever seen standing on a live Tellermine."

Jackson's attitude was, of course, correct, and mine was not. I had been dazzled. Jackson had preserved a realistic sense of proportion.

I see no great harm either in name dropping or in the enjoyment of rubbing shoulders with the great, provided, of course, that a few basic rules are obeyed.

First, then, there must be a sense of proportion, as Jackson had rightly appreciated.

It was a similar sense of proportion that compelled Mr. Groucho Marx to refuse an invitation to join a local club on the grounds that he would not wish to join a club that wanted members such as he.

It is an inverse sense of proportion that impels a certain senior but unsuccessful QC to attend the memorial services of notabilities whether he knew them or not, so that his name may appear in the list of those present and thus remind solicitors that he, on the other hand, is still alive.

The efficient name-dropper must also be a man who knows how to startle. If the conversation turns to cricket you're entitled to repeat the fine argument you once had in the pavilion at Lord's with Jack Hobbs, but this will score no more than five out of ten because it's not all that unexpected. If, on the other hand, you can relate truthfully and at first hand what the Pope told you about his intention of forming a cricket eleven out of the Vatican Guard, then you're home and dry.

The trouble is that to drop a name well also requires an element of luck.

When I was up at Oxford I used to play Schubert's Trio Opus 99, No 1 in B Flat with Einstein and a nice but rather spotty historian from Burgess Hill whose name I'm afraid I've forgotten. Hitler had thrown Einstein out and Christ Church, where I was then *in stat pup*, had welcomed him in. He played the violin nearly as badly as I played the 'cello, but far worse than Burgess Hill played the piano. We were neighbours in Canterbury Quad and we used to foregather of an evening and have an ill-balanced but enjoyable bash. I also owned a canary which, as canaries will, bestirred himself when we were in full blast and contributed an ear-splitting descant. Our enjoyment was not shared by one of our neighbours, Sir Roy Harrod, a distinguished economist but a canarophobe. My scout, the faithful Quelch, had already warned us that Sir Roy was about to complain to the Senior Censor that my canary seed was luring mice into his bathroom, and that in his (Quelch's) opinion Schubert, coming on top of all this, was not much likely to help. It was here that Einstein proved his

144

worth. Attack, he reminded me, was the best form of defence. Before any complaint could be lodged I should wait upon the Senior Censor (Prof. Gilbert Ryle, the distinguished philosopher, and equally canarophobic) in order to protest that Sir Roy's frightful mice were stealing my poor little canary's rations and what was he going to do about it? I sought an interview. Both the two sages were unhinged by the stark purity of my argument. And when I added that none other than Prof. Albert Einstein was endorsing the logic of my cause, my succés was palpably fou.

This ploy made the grade on two out of three counts. The shock-tactic was overwhelming and the name-dropping had the additional merit of truth. Where it let me down, of course, was in the difficulty it has presented of working it into the conversation with ease and conviction on subsequent occasions. I must emphasise that this is an essential feature of name-dropping. The Hobbs in the pavilion gambit conforms to the rules, but the element of surprise is lacking. Since, however, cricket tends to crop up in any civilised conversation, you can always introduce Jack Hobbs and score a moderate success. How often though, are you likely to be involved in a conversation in which mice, Einstein, canaries, and Sir Roy Harrod will all suddenly slide into place? Incidentally, this is also a good reason for not taking up the 'cello. If you play the piano and want to show off, you will eventually find a stool to which you can sidle and a piano lid which you can, to the resigned encouragement of the company, shyly lift. It's not so easy, however, to clear your throat and say you'll just slip up to your room and see if your man has remembered to put in your 'cello.

Of course, for real shock tactics a bad name can be even more effectively dropped than a good one. This is an undeveloped ploy. You have dined poorly and the subject of poisoning crops up. "Dr. Crippen?" you observe. "Why yes, of course. One of my grandfather's oldest and dearest friends. A most polished and

145

resourceful chap." Later, when the port is circulating the criminal ebullience of our age is under discussion "The train robbers?" you casually remark, "Knew all of 'em well. In my regiment of course. Ingenious lot. Introduced C Troop to the art of safe-blowing. The BQMS was very impressed and laid on a course for our national service intake."

Sometimes there are names good and bad which one would like to drop, could drop, but hesitates to drop, and there are famous shoulders which one has rubbed but with only qualified satisfaction.

For Lieutenant-Generals (see above) read Lord Chancellors. In 1942, the year in which my father died and in which I first took my seat in the House of Lords, I knew few Lord Chancellors worth speaking of and fewer still worth speaking to. So I was naturally flattered when an attendant brought me a note from Lord Simon on the Woolsack asking if I was indeed the son of his dear old friend, how did I do, welcome to their Lordships' House and would I meet him in the Princes' Chamber at half past four? I met him. He put his arm around my shoulder and (in defiance of legend) addressed me by my correct name. He then walked me up and down the corridor outside the library and he talked to me for over half an hour. He talked (beautifully, of course) about everything under the sun – ships (which were then of great national importance), shoes (which were heavily rationed), and sealing wax, which I believe was then unobtainable. But what was odd were the things he did not talk about. He never once mentioned his dear old friend, my father. Nor did he ask me how I did, where my regiment was stationed, or what were my views on cabbages and kings. Did the Great Man thereafter dismiss me from his mind? You might think so but you'd be wrong. Ten years later I became engaged to be married and Lord Simon wrote and asked if he could propose our health at my wedding. As we had not even presumed to ask him to the ceremony, this raised a tricky point of protocol. It also annoyed my fiancée's

146

god-father who was to have proposed the toast and had been rehearsing a waggish piece for weeks.

Lord Simon made, as you might expect, a wonderful speech. It was flatteringly urbane, witty and melodious but it lasted for nearly ten minutes. (Still, he *was* Lord Simon.) Some weeks later I met him by chance outside his room in the Lords and I thanked him warmly, and I hope sincerely, for what he had done. I said I was sorry (and I meant this) that there had been no shorthand writer present at our wedding to take down his winged words for the benefit of our grandchildren. He said that this omission could be rectified immediately. He took me into his room. For a moment I imagined he was going to open a file and hand me the script of his speech. He did nothing of the sort. He summoned a secretary and immediately dictated the address he had given at 6 Stanhope Gate on May 8, 1951 without deviating, as far as I could see, by so much as a comma from his original masterpiece. A kind man and, I think, a better man than some historians may allow; but a puzzling man. So I do not drop his name without, if this be physically possible, a faint raising of the eyebrow.

But Lord Simon is dead. So is John the Baptist and I always irreverently link their names when I remember that the first Rotarian was the first man to call John the Baptist, Jack.

Do, I wonder, the rules of the Elysian Fields conform to the accepted and earthly rules of name-dropping?

I have always been an admirer of Helen of Troy. She was a buxom little piece; refined but noticeable – the Diana Dors of the Dardanelles, and I am sorry that Robert Graves has treated her so harshly. When Madame Arcati summoned her blithe spirit to embarrass poor Mr. Condamine, I was enchanted to hear that she had (in Miss Kay Hammond's blissfully plummy contralto) been playing backgammon with Helen of Troy; and found her rather fun. I'm so glad. I shall take up backgammon when I die.

I once heard Winston say (and you may call him Winston even if you never knew him, but you mustn't call Mountbatten "Dickie" unless you do) – well, I once heard Winston say he hoped that on reaching heaven he would be vouchsafed a short conversation with the first Duke of Marlborough in order to clear up a few technical points for the next edition of the book, and he then hoped to be able to enjoy a conversation with His Grace and Dr. Johnson on the subjects of brandy, high toryism, and the declining behaviour of bargees on the River Thames. I should love to listen in on that. But it will, alas, as a conversation, lack the one thing that any connoisseur of name-dropping would welcome with open arms. I'm afraid that nobody in that company is likely to drop mine.

26

Dictatorial Bees

"Power crazy, that's what you are," said the little old lady in the black straw toque, angrily shaking her umbrella at me from the back of the hall. "Lusting for power, just like the rest of them."

I felt a little hurt by this. In point of fact, all I was doing was standing in the Conservative interest in the Montagu Square Ward of the Marylebone Borough Council, where the opportunities for power-craziness are, frankly, limited. At a later date, I did manage to dissuade my colleagues from building an infants' crêche in the middle of the busiest traffic intersection in the borough, but even Mother Toque could hardly have detected the Dictator's hand in that.

On reflection, I should perhaps have mentioned in my speech that my wish to enter public life was not prompted by any wild lust for power, or even by the desire to achieve great things. All I wanted to do was to stop other people from doing damn silly ones.

Lindsay Anderson announced the other day that if he were made Dictator he'd have two main objectives. He'd abolish television and he'd insist that every child in this country should have a classical education. I go along with him some of the way. Television, I feel, is for appearing on, and not for watching. And the chief benefit I have derived from a classical education is the ability to contemplate with a lofty disdain the fortune it has prevented me from amassing.

Nevertheless, if I were made Dictator tomorrow my conduct would be more aggressively negative than that of Mr. Anderson. I don't just want to put the clock back. I want another clock.

The trouble with this country is not that we are badly governed, but that we are disastrously over-governed. There are too many Acts of Parliament, too many by-laws, too many Royal Commissions, too much supervision and too many do-gooders busily making matters worse. Leave well alone, say I; or (as Nanny used to say) if you pick it, it'll never heal.

I wouldn't, however, go so far as to do away with Parliament, although it's always amused me that the only two statues standing within the curtilage of the Palace of Westminster are those of Richard I, who never summoned Parliament and Oliver Cromwell, who tried to abolish it. So although the country is never better governed than when Parliament is not sitting, I myself wouldn't actually abolish it. I think, however, I'd release the Commons on indefinite leave and hand over the nation's business to the Lords. Much more sensible, much more kindly and not always fretting about the effects of Clause 3(2)a on the floating vote in Lower Bogford.

We'd have to pass a few laws, of course. We'd still have to pay the Army and, naturally, me; but apart from that, the less legislation the better. And do not let us forget the Locrians of Ancient Greece. If any one of them proposed a new law, he was made to stand in the market place of Locris with a rope around his neck, while his project was debated. If a majority approved of his measure, well and good. If not, he was immediately hanged.

And while we are on the subject of majorities, my Dictatorship and I will pay much more attention to the sensible many, and much less to the lunatic few. In the new universities, for example (of which there are far too many) most students still wish to study but they, unfortunately, are not newsworthy. Those who wish to shout and scream or set fire to the Dean are attractive to sub-editors, so they will have to leave at once, never to return. Students who do well and take their degrees will be duly photographed by the media, but not the shouters and screamers.

Too much of our legislation is drafted on the assumption that half the population are knaves and the other half fools. If you spend too much time trying to protect fools from their folly, you will eventually fill the world with fools. If you assume that most men are honest and wish to obey a reasonable and comprehensible law, you obviously run the risk of a few rogues knocking holes in the law. You will also, however, save much time and money which would be better employed elsewhere even though you will probably bankrupt a lot of lawyers and accountants. And every time one of my judges pronounces as unintelligible a law that affects the individual, my strong-arm men will give the draftsman a rope and a sharp prod towards the market place.

Nor shall I waste too much time on petty criminals. If football fans wish to behave like deranged baboons, by all means let them do so. We will close the gates of the stadium, withdraw the police and let them fight it out amongst themselves. The winners may have to walk home because I shall have cancelled all the special trains. British Rail are deep enough in the red as it is without the Arsenal supporters smashing all the light bulbs and ripping up the seats.

If any of these football fans, preferring to return home by car, should drive more carelessly, dangerously or drunkenly than I permit, he won't get just the routine nine months without the option. He'll get three years in gaol, but only at the weekends. He'll still be able to do his job and prevent his family from becoming a burden on the State and he can spend his mid-week evenings discussing with other Arsenal supporters the pros and cons of 150 consecutive weekends in Wandsworth Gaol.

It will, I hope, be agreed that I am not seeking to put the clock back. I don't actually want to revive bear-baiting or cock-fighting, nor the ducking stool, advantageous though that might be for those Women's Libbers who persist in trespassing on my lib. The return of the stocks also has its attractions, particularly for the detention of defaulting tour operators, unidentifiable landlords and people who leave their burglar alarms ringing from dusk till dawn.

Nevertheless, mine will be a benevolent dictatorship. Parliament has always tried to legislate for the reasonable man. We seem, however, to have done it in such a way that the chief beneficiary is too often the unreasonable man, the vandal, the hooligan, the subverter, the disrupter, the drug-addict, the pervert and the general professional nuisance. I think Democracy has given in too often to the tyranny of the Unreasonable man.

The first principles, therefore, of my dictatorship will be to put him down; to remove him from the public view.

On the wall of our town hall there was recently chalked an appealing slogan, "Keep Britain beautiful," it ran, "put your head in a bag."

My men are already out requisitioning all the bags they can lay their hands on.

27
Growing old disgracefully

I am not, I'm afraid, a regular reader of *Le Petit Marocain*. A few weeks ago, however, while on business in Tangier, I came across in that distinguished newspaper a report which made me realise how much I had been missing. Some tough old Moroccan entrepreneur was celebrating his hundredth birthday and had been asked, in the traditional way, to give the press the recipe for his longevity. "Adultery," he declared stoutly. "Adultery, and plenty of the best French brandy."

As an admirer of the best French brandy, I appreciate this attitude. It emphasises the fact that one's approach to old age is relative. I myself acknowledged that I had already reached middle age when I found I was no longer trying to resist temptation, but was only wondering if I had actually missed any. I'm always frightened that it may be my last chance. Consequently, I burden my children with sound but prosaic advice by way of consolation for the fact that I may soon be unable to set them a bad example.

They, for their part, adopt a pitying attitude towards my approaching senility. I have ceased to be square, and am now frankly grotty. French children, faced with the problem of parental decrepitude, address their elders as *Les Ecroulants* – the crumbling ones – from which humiliating status it is but a short step to PPH (*Passeront pas l'hiver*). Age, as I say, is relative, and I still believe that no man is really old until his mother stops worrying about him. The attitude of his children is less disinterested.

If age is relative, then George Bernard Shaw, who

was still an *enfant terrible* in his nineties, has aged considerably since his death. Verdi composed *Falstaff* when he was well into his eighties, and then danced a little jig after its first performance. Our plumber, however, can't stand for office in the local branch of his union because he'll be fifty next birthday.

And what about all those Caucasian worthies, aged one hundred and thirty, whose photographs were displayed in the coloured supplements a few months ago? True or false? I personally think the whole thing was a spoof. I don't believe any one of them was a day over one hundred and twenty. They, however, were mostly soldiers, and we know that old soldiers never die, they simply fade away: a theory that is discomforting to any soldier who after a few years of retirement has tried to get into his old uniform.

The advent of age affects us all differently. Take theatricals, for instance. Some actors like Cary Grant and Rex Harrison are clearly immortal. Pop-group leaders look, sound and smell as though they were all about ninety-four – but I believe that most of them are only seventeen. Actresses, being women, are more difficult. I suppose that the only time a woman wishes she was a year older is when she is having a baby. But when they aren't, actresses stop for a long time at twenty-nine, then suddenly become seventy, and start giving tolerable imitations of Marie Tempest, which makes things confusing for you, me and the insurance companies.

What about the other professions? Soldiers may fade away but some do it very noisily. Doctors go quietly. Retired quantity surveyors and superannuated average adjusters stay well away from the headlines. Huntercombe Golf Course is bunker deep in elderly naval architects and aged conveyancers who rely upon their pensions and their savings, rather than the sale of their clients' confidence, to sustain an appropriate supply of pink gin in their old age.

But soldiers, as I say, are different. They bombard us with their awkwardly ghosted memoirs. I don't myself know any military ghost writers or how they pass their time when they are not, through their principals, waging war with other ghost writers. But I wonder why old soldiers waste so much time fighting all over again the battles that are past, and make so little contribution to the tactics and the strategy of the future. What a pity the Army does not produce more Slessors or more Roskills. Let us, however, be thankful for small mercies. Monty and the controversy his decisions aroused has kept more publishers in business than any other man since Boswell.

Judges also go quietly. They are now compulsorily retired at the age of seventy-five, and nicely pensioned, too. They used to hold office *dum se bene gesserint*. There is something about the contemplative calm of the judicial bench (and the perfectly splendid holidays) that encourages longevity. This carries a useful lesson for restive people like the Beatles. At any rate, a lot of judges in days gone by gesserinted themselves well into their eighties. And, whilst, in their own opinion, their judgement and faculties remained faultless, unsuccessful litigants may sometimes have thought otherwise. In this class I include the estranged couple whose matrimonial affairs were once being discussed at Leeds Assizes before a retired Indian judge sitting as a Divorce Commissioner. Sleep overcame His Lordship after luncheon and, awakening suddenly and guiltily, he observed "Shocking case, shocking. A hundred lashes each". The press reaction was jaundiced.

Businessmen have to ask permission of the stockholders if they want to remain on the board of their company after the statutory age of seventy. This is usually granted because those stockholders who have the patience to read the small print in the annual report and also the time to turn up at the AGM, are round about seventy themselves. Politicians, even the most eminent, have to persuade their constituency associations that there is life in them still at eighty. But it takes a Shinwell, or better still a Churchill, to get away with this; to persuade a selection committee to adopt a man over fifty is difficult, and for a woman frankly impossible.

Si Jeunesse savait, si Viellesse pouvait. The House of Lords, fortunately, gets the best of both worlds. In the nature of things (though to a lot of people's surprise), it contains many more young members than are to be found in the Commons. But it also provides a platform for those wise old birds whom the Spartans would probably have booted over the cliff, but to whom their Lordships listen with pleasure and profit. So, between the wars, did the French Chamber, where they placed a greater premium on old age than they do today. In these days, of course, France changes her governments less frequently than of old. In the thirties, a French elder statesman once dozed off during a critical debate, and awoke to find that he had been Prime Minister twice.

Max Beerbohm, in one of the remarkable broadcasts he gave in his own old age asked why it was that women grow old so much less vulgarly than men. I'm not sure he was right, but he made his point with a poignant lyric–

Uncle, back from Evensong,
Rang for Cook, and did her wrong.
"Herbert, I'm surprised," said Auntie,
Catching Uncle in flagrante.
"There's a proper time for gaieties,
But please remember, dear, what day it is."

He went on to blame the doctors and the scientists who by their skill have thrown the relativity of age out of balance. In India, a widow is decrepit at thirty, as a result of poverty, malnutrition and disease. Here, thanks to the successful campaigns waged against TB, diphtheria and smallpox, the announcement pages of the newspapers are full of the news of golden weddings. I'm in shipping myself and I welcome this for purely commercial reasons. Many men, when they retire, celebrate their release by travelling round the world, and the best of luck to them, and to all our shareholders as well.

Travel is a far more satisfying relaxation than golf because by the time you've made your fortune and can afford to lose a lot of golf balls, you aren't able to hit them far enough for it to matter.

One thing really worries me about growing old. More than a million old people in Britain live alone. Some, of course, are not completely alone, and by no means all are poor. Most of them have the telly. Many have children to ring them up. Others, less fortunate, only have the WVS to call, or the local authority to ask tactful and kindly questions at clinically regular intervals. I know a bit about this because I was once chairman of our borough's public health committee and it was my job to ask the questions. No matter how persuasive these questions are, there are still a lot of old people who ought to be in a home, but intend, come what may, to stay in their own. They can be poorer than church mice and sicker, but unless they actually come within the terms of section sixteen of the Act you can't force them to leave, and one day they'll be found on the kitchen floor dead (ten days dead) and you wonder what good you're doing in local government. Age is relative; pride is not.

I am now past middle-age. Youth looks forward, old age looks back and middle-age merely looks startled. I don't know whether the reporter from *Le Petit Marocain* asked his centenarian any other impertinent questions – about his triumphs, his regrets and his views on the bomb, the mini-skirt, or the balance of payments. I don't know what I shall think when I'm one hundred, or, indeed, whether I shall be able to think at all. But in my mid-fifties I always thought that the principal pleasure of middle-age was looking back at some of the girls one didn't marry.

Shakespeare was wrong about the ages of men. There were not seven, there were three – youth, middle age and "My word, you don't look it."

I hope that our Marocain didn't look it any more than I do.

157

28
Pray silence

"Mr. Chairman," roars the Toastmaster, "Your Grace, Your Eminence, Your Beatitude, Your Worships, Aldermen, Sheriffs, My Lords, Ladies and Gentlemen, pray silence for Sir Bert Buggins, Holder of the Ruritanian Order of Chastity Fourth Class, Knight Grand Cross of the Order of St. Tom, St. Dick and St. Harry, and Prime Warden of the Worshipful Company of Rathole Bunger-Uppers, who will propose the Toast to the Guests."

Our Bert, who's been waiting twenty years for this occasion, clambers unsteadily to his feet, blows into the microphone to see if it's working, prays to heaven he'll be able to remember at least some of that gullet-busting preamble, and launches into his carefully prepared impromptu speech.

Behind him the Toastmaster pulls Bert's chair back, drapes an immaculate white glove over an immaculate red sleeve, and does his best to look amused at Bert's halting version of the story about the Christian, the lion, and the after-dinner speech which he is now hearing for the seven hundred and forty-third time.

The Toastmaster is a singularly British creation. Correction: English. Further correction: London. There are, I believe, a few good Toastmasters lurking in the Provinces, and if the provincials haven't got one handy, the R.S.M. from the local Territorial Regiment may be able to oblige. If things are really desperate, the Headwaiter at the Grand Hotel can probably weigh in with the resounding accents of Barcelona, or Milan, but if you want the job done properly you'd better get a man down from London.

Here you will be faced with a slight problem, for no less than five organisations are eagerly seeking your custom. There's the Society of London Toastmasters, founded in 1950, with twenty-five members; there's also the London Guild of Toastmasters; and finally, there's the Association of Toastmasters & Masters of Ceremonies; there's the Toastmasters & M.C.'s Federation; there's the Guild of Professional Toastmasters. And, believe it or not, these five bodies, in toto, embrace scarcely more than a hundred members. One would have thought, therefore, that they would be well advised to get together and pool their talents.

Why do I speak so positively, and what authority have I to do so? I must declare an interest. I was for nearly twenty years, Honorary Toastmaster to the Society of London Toastmasters. I've thoroughly enjoyed the job, I was proud to hold the title, and I've made a lot of very good friends. But enough, I feel, is enough, and I've at last retired.

Not that the work was all that onerous. The most I've had to do is to act as Toastmaster at the Society's annual Christmas dinner; and whilst I have often made a nonsense of this particular task, I have, in turn, been able to note that not all Toastmasters can be classed as brilliant after-dinner speakers. I have also been able to discover why a Toastmaster is a useful man to have around.

The Americans also have Toastmasters, but these are of a different breed. They are chatter-uppers; glad-handers; verbal back-slappers; and their job it is to put an audience on good terms with itself. This is something the Americans dearly love to do, even though the doing of it invariably lengthens the proceedings by at least a couple of hours. When in evening dress, however, the Americans like to proceed slowly.

The British Toastmaster chats nobody up. Not for nothing is *"omnium cum dignitate"* the motto of our Society. Apart from the formalities of announcement, a Toastmaster should never open his mouth, though I do remember one occasion when a Toastmaster was so carried away by a speech about the plight of ex-service pensioners that he seized the microphone from the speaker and launched into a powerful postscript, drawn from his own experiences. The effect was tremendous, but he was never invited to repeat it.

The best way of discovering why a Toastmaster is necessary is to attend a function where the organisers think he's not. The result is invariably a shambles.

We British are a tidy people. We are fond of protocol though we dislike pomposity. We approve of formality but we do not like it to be unnecessarily protracted. Hence the Toastmaster.

The hosts at your dinner have taken much trouble to organise the function. The ladies have put on their prettiest dresses. The chef has done his best with his *Escalopines de Veau St. Jacques.* So why not complete the picture and have a Toastmaster to see that the guests are properly announced, the company correctly marshalled, and the speakers brought to their feet in due order? And if some little local difficulty should crop up – if a waiter should mistakenly spill too much soup over your wife's dress, or Bert Buggins a little too much Scotch into himself – then just pass the word to the Toastmaster and nobody will know that anything is amiss.

Sometimes, a crisis can be more serious. On two occasions, alas, I have known a speaker collapse in the middle of a speech; and on both occasions the Toastmaster, by tact and quickness of wit, managed to avert what might otherwise have been an unhappy scene.

How do you get hold of a Toastmaster? If you don't yourself know a Toastmaster personally, discuss the matter with the Banqueting Manager of any big hotel. He probably has a pet Toastmaster whom he'll recommend. But there's no hard-and-fast rule about this, and no closed shop. Ring up, then, any Toastmaster you like. His wife will invariably answer the 'phone. That's her job. If her husband doesn't happen to be free on that particular night, she'll give you the name of the next man down the list. They work to an agreed rota. There are now even one or two lady Toastmistresses, and I hope their husbands do the same for them in reverse, but goodness knows how the bachelors get on.

How did Toastmasters originate? Their history is hazy. The first Toastmaster was, I suppose, Stentor the Herald. Skipping a few centuries, we learn that at Edward II's first State Banquet, the official announcements were made by his favourite, Piers de Gaveston, about whom the less said the better. At George IV's Coronation Breakfast, the job was done by the Earl Marshal, who was subsequently found behind a dirty linen-basket drunk (I'm afraid) as a lord. And, believe it or not, the poet Robbie Burns was once a Toastmaster. But, by and large, the Toastmaster as we now know him is a comparatively modern invention.

How do you become a Toastmaster? In former days, quite a few of them appear to have been unsuccessful baritones on Eastbourne Pier, but now they're a more professional lot. Some are the sons of Toastmasters. Some are coming up through the trainee ranks of the catering trade. This is as it should be, because there is a close connection between Toastmaster, Banqueting Manager, Headwaiter and Chef. A few Toastmasters are ex-headwaiters, civic macebearers, or beadles of City Livery Companies. In all cases, new candidates are – in our lot, at any rate – rigorously vetted.

How much do they earn? I've never had the effrontery to ask. A successful man might do a trade-show in the morning, followed by a business luncheon at mid-day; then a cocktail-party in the West End, and a City banquet in the evening. Even so, the fees are not princely, and the wear and tear on white ties and red coats, must be dreadful. Not all Toastmasters, of course, are as busy as that. Some have other jobs during the day, in Directors' lunch-rooms and the like. One of our members winds the clocks in the Head Office of a big foreign bank, and he says that it's driving him mad. But most of them work full-time and are rarely back home in Northwood before dawn.

There are naturally horses for courses. Some Toastmasters specialise in Masonic and Rotary work. Others are popular in the Jewish community. Some, I'm sorry to say, will put on funny hats and do "Knees up, Mother Brown". All can judge when a full and flowery treatment is in order, or when slightly less protocol would fill the bill.

And talking of bills, I remember that the Toastmaster who officiated at my stepdaughter's wedding forgot to send in his. I wrote in due course and asked him to let me know what I owed him. "Nothing," he replied. His services were his personal wedding-present to the bride and bridegroom.

They're a very nice body of men, these Toastmasters, and I envy my successor.

29
Souvenirs

I think that the American gentleman who bought London Bridge as a souvenir and plonked it down in the middle of Arizona had all the right ideas. And London Bridge has all the right qualifications for the perfect souvenir. It is handsome, it is unusual, and since there appears to be no water in Arizona it is also completely useless.

Indeed, I can only think of one other souvenir in the same class, and that was the baby alligator which was given to my Uncle Eustace as he was leaving a party of Bright Young Things in the spring of 1927. He took it home to his flat in Albany and put it in the bath. Next morning the alligator was still there, though looking understandably peaky. My Uncle's man-servant, however, had gone, leaving a note on the kitchen dresser. "Sir," it read, "I cannot work for a gentleman who keeps baby alligators in his bath. I would have mentioned this when you engaged me but I never thought it was likely to arise."

Into the more orthodox class of souvenirs there falls a wide range of plastic Guardsmen, sticky pink rock with "Blackpool" written all through, and delicately-wrought dolls' tea-sets proclaiming that they are a present from Budleigh Salterton. About all such items there have been complaints both as to suitability and as to design.

Ever vigilant, the Council of Industrial Design mounted an exhibition which demonstrated convincingly that it's just as easy to design a good-looking plastic Guardsman as a bad one. The Council, however, did not convince everybody that a plastic Guardsman, even if designed by Lord Snowdon himself, is what we really want. Is this the image of the dynamic, pragmatic, gritty, nuclear-orientated Britain that we would like our visitors to take home and display on the mantlepieces of Kimberley and Kalamazoo?

Well, it may not be what *we* want, but, unfortunately, it appears to be what the tourists want. You try selling them scale model manganese gudgeon sprockets or elegantly framed mezzotints of Didcot power station, and see where that gets you.

We're expecting 15 per cent more tourists this year than last; and it therefore looks as if London in August is going to contain more tourists than natives. There's even talk of Changing the Guard twice daily. I personally am against this. It is, after all, the Palace and not the Palladium. But is any enterprising coach operator planning package tours to sunny Harwell, or arranging escorted outings to British Leyland? I think not. It'll be the same old circuit as ever; the Crown Jewels and Stratford, Windermere and Windsor Castle, and Laurence Olivier if anyone can fiddle some tickets. And why not? That's the state of the market. That's what our visitors come for, and its models of the Crown Jewels and their guardian Beefeaters (sorry, Yeomen Warders) that they'll want to take home, not to mention tea-cloths with pictures of the Tower and (if they know the right shop in the Kings Road) ladies' frilly garters with the Royal Borough's Coat of Arms embroidered on one side and "Fix thy thoughts on things above" on the other. (The same emporium used to sell knickers made out of the Stars and Stripes until the American Embassy protested, and quite right, too.)

On the other hand, I suspect that the progress of science must be making serious inroads into these branches of the souvenir trade. Amateur photography has now become more professional than can be good for the future of the postcard industry. A stereo record of Trooping the Colour brings back more vivid memories than a thousand plastic Guardsmen. The tape recorder is also here to stay.

Perhaps science can help us further still. I was telling you about my Uncle Eustace. Well, he eventually steadied up and married Auntie Hetty who survived him by many years. On the end of her drawing-room sofa she kept a little rubber air cushion upon which nobody was allowed to bounce. We children always understood that it contained poor Uncle's dying breath. Now here's the germ of a useful idea. Before the Six-days War the Israelis used to do a lively trade in bottled Jordan water. So what about bottled Heathrow fog, or dehydrated Centre Court rain pills to be reactivated when you return to Tallahassie, Fla., and want to describe your European trip to all the lovely people back home?

The trouble is, of course, that the souvenirs we would really like our visitors to take home are always the most difficult to put together. I live in a small village in the Cotswolds. This weekend we've had an American friend to stay, and the weather's been really lovely. This is just as well because the last time he was over the weather was vile and he went home complaining that the English base their domestic heating arrangements on an exaggerated confidence in the Almighty, the Gulf Stream and two small lumps of Coalite.

Last Sunday, however, restored his faith in the English climate. The cherry blossom was at its best, the cuckoo was shouting its silly head off, and the bees were about their business. The church tower was solid gold in the morning sunlight. Our guest sat under the lilac on the lawn drinking Pimms No. 1, on the composition of which I had just delivered a scholarly teach-in. "This is it," he said, sweeping his arm round our garden, "I'll take all this back as a souvenir. Wrap it up for me at once. Never mind your plastic Guardsmen. You can keep your Anne Hathaway Cottage tea-cosies. Away with your phallic glass tubes of Alum Bay coloured sand. Just wrap this all up for me and I'll take it back to

Chicago." "Very good, Sir," I replied, "and would there be anything else?"

He paused reflectively, "Yes," he said, "there is. You can slip in Princess Anne, Marks & Spencer, and Question Time in the House of Commons."

I must see what I can do

30

My Father

When the Carlton Club was bombed in 1941, Quintin Hogg carried his aged father, Lord Hailsham, out of the rubble, just as Aeneas, some years before, had carried his father, Anchises, from the ruins of Troy.

My own father and I were also members of the Carlton and had we been present on that May evening I hope I should have been prompted by the same filial piety. My task, however, would have been onerous because my father was a heavy man. He once had a horse faint under him whilst hunting with the Devon and Somerset and he had not grown any lighter as the years went by. His weight, however, was not due to gluttony for he was an abstemious man. He had suffered a serious accident in the twenties and this prevented him from taking much exercise from then onwards. He had gone down to Torquay to speak in support of the local MP, Charlie Williams, whose loquacity had not unnaturally earned him the nick-name of Talkie Williams. My father slipped whilst strolling in the garden after the meeting and broke his leg. The break never healed properly. It eventually gave him phlebitis and the clot went to his eyes so that towards the end of his days he was almost blind.

The accident also put an end to his morning ride in the Row. He kept two horses in the mews behind our home in Montagu Square. He had bought the house for his mother in 1907 when she came down from Norwich to join him in London. I was born in the same room as that in which she died. All my own children were born in the same room, too. I doubt if there are many Londoners who can say that.

He was also, I think, the last MP to ride down on horse-back to the House of Commons to take his seat. He entered the House in 1918 and went up to the Lords in 1937. When I took my own seat in the Lords after his death in 1942, I remember one of the older policemen telling me that as a young officer, he used to hold my father's chestnut mare Vanity as he climbed down onto the mounting block that in those days stood outside Westminster Hall. He would also help him pull off his spurs which were not allowed to be worn inside the House.

My father had made two previous attempts to enter Parliament, fighting the difficult Manchester seat of Stretford in 1910 and 1912. His political mentor was Sir William Joynson-Hicks (known as Jix), who subsequently became Home Secretary. Jix lived at the end of Montagu Square and one day, in, I think, the year 1908, my father went along to keep an appointment with him, only to find that Jix was in bed with 'flu and closeted with his doctor. The doctor happened to have his daughter with him and as it was a cold day, she had been summoned from their carriage to warm herself in the waiting room.

This delayed appointment did not unduly displease my father because the doctor's daughter proved to be an extremely pretty girl and my father, who was not a shy man, engaged her in lively conversation. This, however, was not a success and ended in a sharp quarrel which was not finally patched up until 19th December 1912 when they were married at the West London Synagogue in Upper Berkeley Street. Her family came of Quaker stock but my mother bravely converted to Judaism. Her parents refused to come to the wedding.

Despite the fact that there was a difference of nearly fifteen years in their ages and they had very little in common, their marriage was extremely happy.

My mother liked dancing and parties and the theatre all of which, I suspect, my father regarded as works of the devil. To call him an intolerant man would, of course, be unfilial but I'm afraid that it would also be true. He knew he was sadly at fault in this respect but I only realised it a short while before he died when he suddenly poured out to me his shame at his failure to meet my mother even half way in her innocent fondness for dancing and parties and the theatre. Happily, my father also thought that the sun rose and set out of the back of my mother's head, and during the twenty seven years of her widowhood a day scarcely passed when she didn't talk about him with pride and affection.

Constant pain in his later years obviously did little to detract from his eccentricities. Nor did his harsh upbringing do much to encourage gaiety, even in an ambitious and talented young man.

He was born in Norwich in 1872, into a tight-knit and old-established Jewish community. There had been a synagogue in Norwich from time immemorial. Its congregation came and went; Edward III and Cromwell left their mark as they also left their mark on the other ancient Jewish communities in York and Lincoln. Norwich, however, could also remember that some of their community had achieved unenviable fame by being charged with the murder of the young St. William of Norwich. Our ancestors were eventually exonerated by the Judges of the King's Bench, but after, not before, they had all been duly burnt at the stake.

Our family records are hazy, as most Jewish records in England inevitably must be, but the authorities think we have been established in Norwich for a very long time.

The leading families in my father's day were named Samuel and Haldinstein. My Samuel grandfather was Benjamin, a charming and rather dreamy scholar. He was respected and much loved. He was also extremely good looking. I have a portrait of him by John Joseph Cotman whom he befriended. Half Norwich (if the *Eastern Daily Press* is to be believed) turned out for his funeral. He lived at 43 Timberhill where my father was born. The house is a handsome building with the pointed leucomb windows that are so characteristic of mediaeval Norwich. Until the Arab Boycott forced my dismissal, I used to be the London Chairman of the Norwich Union Insurance Group and from my seat in the board-room of their new Norwich Headquarters, I could look straight down onto the house in which my father was born.

Ben married Rosetta Haldinstein. Her father, Philip, who came originally from Switzerland, was the founder of the family boot and shoe business which still trades under its original name, though taken over by Bally (also of Switzerland) many years ago. Grandfather Ben worked rather half-heartedly for his father-in-law and they never got on. I seldom heard of anyone who did get on with him and Ben's fragile relations with his employer and kinsman became even less cordial after he had come across the old brute one Sunday afternoon with the cook upon his knee.

My father went to Norwich Grammar School, still one of the finest in the country. It was founded (as he never tired of telling me) long before Winchester, where I myself was educated. Amongst his fellow Norvicensians were Nelson, Crome, Cotman, George Borrow and Sir Thomas Browne.

The school, for £14 a year, turned young Arthur Michael Samuel into a first class classical scholar and for this, he never failed to speak of his old Headmaster, Canon Tancock, with affectionate gratitude. My father, in due course, became a Governor of the school and there are memorial tablets to him and his beloved brother Frank on the chapel wall.

When he was fifteen, his father Ben died, suddenly and almost penniless. My father had to leave school at once in order to support his brother and widowed mother. Inevitably, he quarrelled with old grandfather Philip and soon left for London with the proverbial shilling in his pocket, but not before he had grounded himself pretty well in the mysteries of making boots and shoes and selling them thereafter.

I think the next few years must have been hard going and might have been even harder if he had not fallen in with his uncle, Henry Samuel, who kept an antique shop in Oxford Street. By odd co incidence that particular shop is now owned by a fashion group named Wallis of which I myself am Chairman.

He worked successfully enough at selling both boots and antiques to help his brother to Magdalen and eventually to the Chancery Bar. He also began to turn his own thoughts towards politics. Lord Rosebery was a customer of the shop and his eye seems to have lighted favourably upon my father. Rosebery soon took him on as run-around boy, researcher and speech-writer. My father revered Rosebery and kept his photograph on his mantlepiece till the day he died. I have it still. They only quarrelled once and that was when my father became engaged to be married. Rosebery wrote him a cynical and rather callous letter telling him that by character and instinct he was quite unsuited to the married state and had far better seek out an appropriate mistress. Father was not best pleased, nor, indeed, was his fiancée to whom he rather unwisely showed the letter. For some odd reason, neither of them saw fit to destroy it and I have not done so either, if only to satisfy myself that even men of Rosebery's elegance can sometimes make errors of taste.

From 1910 to 1912, Father journeyed regularly up to Stretford to further the Conservative cause. Most of the private papers he kept were lost in the blitz and I have few records of those two campaigns. But the Manchester Conservatives have long memories and they had much to show and tell me when I myself was asked to speak in Stretford in 1947. I was proud of what I was shown and told. Their candidate had not done too badly for a man who by the party standards of those days could look for little support from the social or political establishment. The *Manchester Guardian* called him vigorous but unorthodox and Lord Derby advised him not to introduce so many Greek quotations into his speeches to Lancashire Chambers of Commerce.

In 1912, he received a surprising and flattering invitation. His native City of Norwich asked him to become its next Lord Mayor. Norwich was, and still is, one of the few cities that from time to time elects its first citizen from outside the ranks of its Council Members. This has the advantage of introducing new ideas and a fresh approach. On the other hand, the new Chairman of the City Council has much to learn about the niceties of local politics and personalities. My father had also another obvious disadvantage; he was a bachelor. They said he must get married as soon as possible. He did, though I don't know whether he told the City Fathers that he already had my mother firmly in mind.

(The next bachelor Lord Mayor to be elected in Norwich was an old friend of mine named Tom Eaton, some forty years later. I told him that he must follow my father's example and get married during his year of office. This he duly did and I attended his wedding in the Church of St. Peter Mancroft.)

My father obviously enjoyed his Lord Mayoralty and I like to think that Norwich enjoyed him too, though I don't think they quite realised what had hit them. I have been browsing through the City records. He duly kicked off at the football matches of that distinguished Norwich team, the Canaries; he attended innumerable banquets; he laid foundation stones; presented prizes; complained about the traffic jams on Orford Hill and, out of his own pocket, presented an eye infirmary to the Norfolk and Norwich Hospital. But he also lectured them on the relationship between Ruisdael, Cuyp, Hobbema and the Norwich School of Painting (upon which he was an acknowledged expert) and he scolded them for their neglect of their fellow-citizen George Borrow, his Lavengro, Romany Rye and Wild Wales. He bought Borrow's birth-place, and presented it to the City as a museum, and he commissioned the young A. J. Munnings (later President of the Royal Academy) to draw the cover for the programme of the opening ceremony. At the end of the ceremony, the Sheriff's wife was heard to observe, "Well, it's all very nice, I'm sure, but I must confess I've never heard of this Mr. Burroughs." So much for civic pride.

After the war when, thanks to Hitler, housing was short in Norwich, the City asked me if I would mind if the Borrow Museum could be used to house the homeless. I naturally agreed, guessing that not one person in a hundred would ever visit the place in the role which my father had originally intended.

His native City, however, did not forget him, and in 1928 they elected him an Honorary Freeman. I was given the day off from Winchester to attend the ceremony in St. Andrew's Hall. He made a superb speech in praise of Norwich, its achievements and its place in the history of England. They presented him with a silver model of a Norfolk wherry (which is a cross between a Thames barge and a Dutch bum-boat) and gave my mother a model of one of St. Peter Mancroft's bells mounted as a swinging table-gong. I got nothing and complained about this to the police inspector who was standing behind my chair. A few weeks later, the post brought me a set of cuff-links made out of four buttons from the sleeve of a Norwich policeman's uniform. I am wearing them now, as I write.

Shortly before he became Lord Mayor my father had published his first book – a study of the life and work of Giovanni Battista Piranesi, the great Italian architectural draughtsman. Today Piranesi is well known and well appreciated but in 1910, despite his association with Robert Adam, he was almost unheard of. The book was kindly received by the critics and went to a second edition in 1912. That edition, unlike the first, carried a dedication – "To Phoebe". The book remained the standard work for many years. In 1923 he published a book on the Herring and its effect on British history, and in 1928 a monograph on the working of the Bill of Exchange which ran to three editions.

An even wider range of taste and knowledge is

revealed in the essays he contributed to the old *Saturday Review* from 1918 to 1923. They covered such diverse subjects as Norwich Shawls, Historical Bastards, Apples and *Religio Medici*. All this suggests a voracious appetite for reading and this indeed was so. The librarians of both Houses of Parliament, St. Marylebone Public Library and the Carlton Club all became familiar with his tastes. These were largely historical. The only novel which I think he really enjoyed was *Clochemerle*. He enjoyed Gibbon's *Decline and Fall* much more, not to mention J.A. Symonds', *Italy and the Renaissance* and Hodgkin's *Italy and her Invaders* – twenty-three volumes in all, which he read from cover to cover.

He passed on to me his fascination with the Italian Renaissance and we travelled much together in Italy. I once even felt moved to launch out on a comparative study of Lorenzo the Magnificent and the other princes of the Renaissance. How, for instance, would Caesar Borgia have shaped up to Henry VIII and François Premier? Unfortunately, whenever I've set pen to paper some genuine scholar has come up with almost exactly the same idea.

My father, of course, wrote nothing during the war. He was too old to serve in the Armed Forces so he worked with the Special Constabulary at night, and on dial sights and other optical equipment at the Ministry of Munitions during the day. My own earliest memory is of my father carrying me down to the cellars below Montagu Square during an air raid. I remember watching the searchlight beams through the landing window as they swept the sky and I remember listening to the boy-scouts' bugles sounding the all-clear. I could not have been more than three at the time.

In the 1918 General Election he was returned as Conservative MP for the Farnham division of Surrey and served them faithfully until he went to the Lords in 1937. He refused to take a house in the Constituency because he wished to avoid getting mixed up in dustbin politics. This, he said, was the job of the Borough Council.

In 1924, after only six years in the House, he was moved on to the Front Bench as Minister for Overseas Trade and later in 1927 promoted to the Treasury as Financial Secretary. The DOT was a hybrid department. Its Minister answered both to the Foreign Office (where Sir Austen Chamberlain was then in charge) and to the Board of Trade where Sir Philip Cunliffe-Lister (later Lord Swinton) was President. He was immensely able but not immensely popular. Whilst my father was lying abed with his broken leg, Cunliffe-Lister proposed the abolition of my father's Department. Baldwin, then Prime Minister, would have none of it, neither would Parliament, and the office and Father remained, though on cooler terms with the President of the Board of Trade than hitherto.

At the Treasury, my father answered (if that be the right word) to Winston who was Chancellor of the Exchequer. I have had a look at some of the records and I would have said that the Chancellor and his Financial Secretary went much their own way. I would also say that my father knew more about the complexities of high finance than he did about the complexities of Winston Churchill.

Altogether he was in office for over five years. The late Sir Edward Crowe (father of Sir Colin Crowe, himself a distinguished Civil Servant) was one of his Permanent Secretaries. I remember a conversation with him shortly before he died and he told me that my father, of whom he was obviously fond, was an efficient and knowledgeable Minister, well liked and respected both by his Civil Servants and the House of Commons. When I myself started to play an active part in House of Lords affairs after the war, I was happy to find how many old colleagues of his on both sides of both Houses spoke well of him and told me how often he had gone out of his way to be helpful to younger Members. They also went out of their way to refer to him by his nickname of Arthur Michael. He would have liked that. I certainly did.

175

After the landslide election of 1931 he remained on the back benches where I think he was really happier than he had been in office. He was certainly kept pretty busy. He was (like most ex-Financial Secretaries) appointed Chairman of the Public Accounts Committee and served on many other Committees that were particularly concerned with Trade and Finance. Indeed, *Punch* was moved to publish a clerihew about him under an excellent caricature by A.W. Lloyd, their political artist:–

Sir Arthur Michael Samuel has spent pretty
Nearly all his life in committee
It cannot therefore have been easy
To find time to write a life of Piranesi.

After he became a Member of the House of Lords, he seems to have taken an active part in the business of that House, too. Unfortunately, I never heard him make a Parliamentary speech. I believe, however, that, although he was not an outstanding orator, he was a persuasive and attractive speaker who was often put up to resolve an awkward situation.

He never heard me speak, either, at least, not since I was a small boy. When I came rushing back from some expedition and started to gabble out a description of what I had seen, he would interrupt me gently. "Not too fast, old boy," he would say. "Now look. Call in Nanny and your mother and cousin Jane and Turner" (his secretary and later mine). Robert Turner served us jointly for over sixty years, breaking that service only to deal with the Kaiser and Hitler, and to serve a year's stint as Mayor of Ealing. "Get up on that stool and begin slowly". "Ladies and gentlemen, I've just come back from the Zoo and there I saw . . ." These were my first lessons in public speaking and I have never forgotten them.

In 1934 he underwent a serious abdominal operation. His health steadily declined and being forced to leave Montagu Square by the blitz was the last straw. Everything started to go awry and he died quietly on 17th

August 1942, my mother's birthday. He was buried in the Jewish Cemetery at Norwich next to his parents, and my mother's name was added to his headstone in December 1969.

To catalogue the details of a father's career from a fairly good memory, helped by the usual works of reference and the promptings of old friends, is not too difficult. To assess the character and impressions that a father leaves on even the loyalest of sons is a different matter.

He was a man of extraordinary contrasts. For a boy who had left school penniless before his fifteenth birthday, he had achieved much and come far. He was an immensely well-read, cultured man; widely travelled, a decent linguist, a fine horseman and a better than average pianist. He liked the good things of life; he was an excellent judge of claret, cigars, water colours, Johan Sebastian Bach and after-dinner conversation, all helped by a Rabelesian sense of humour.

And yet he was a puritan and a very awkward, quirky one at that. He was aggressively intolerant of loose living and moral sloppiness and he set great score by the old-fashioned concept of *noblesse oblige*. Thus he was not, I'm afraid, an easy-going man and for this I blame those harsh early days and, more practically, an unnaturally low blood pressure which often leads to low spirits.

He could, to put it bluntly, be very difficult. He refused, for instance, to accept any wedding presents, which can hardly have pleased his friends and relations nor indeed my poor mother and she, as I have indicated, had already much to put up with.

He was also, and this worried us, accident-prone. He was out cubbing one day and had gone into a pub for a snack. On the way out he trod heavily on a by-stander's toe. "Beg pardon," said my father, rather too casually. The treadee took the matter less casually. "Beg pardon won't do," he said fiercely. "You're going to have a punch on the snoot." It took the habitués of the King's

Head quite a while to prise the two of them apart.

And who but my father could have got himself locked into the cloakroom at the frontier station on his way back from representing HMG at a League of Nations meeting in Geneva? He was finally hauled, puffing and panting, onto the much-delayed Mitropa express only to find that he had left his top-secret briefcase behind, with the key helpfully tied to the handle.

One Sunday in the Ritz-Carlton in Montreal he went out of the room to pick up the papers and let the door slam behind him, leaving him standing stark-naked in the passage. There were many other such disasters.

I learned a lot from my father's absent-mindedness and, to the annoyance of my family, have become so over-meticulous myself that we invariably reach an airport in time to catch the plane before the one upon which we are booked. I learned a lot else from him and, old-fashioned as I am, I remember it with affectionate gratitude, even those lessons which I didn't actually accept.

He brought me up in the Jewish faith and that is one thing I certainly did accept. His own Judaism was based on loyalty and sentiment rather than on any strictly orthodox beliefs. He went to synagogue as often as he could and was always happy when I went with him. He never failed to recall with gratitude my mother's courage in converting to Judaism at the time of their marriage.

When he left his Stretford constituency in 1912, his supporters and well-wishers presented him with his portrait painted by Solomon J. Solomon RA. It's a fine piece of work and also, so my mother told me, an excellent likeness. It hangs above my table now and looks down at me as I write. It portrays a handsome, burly man with a quizzical, sardonic expression. What he thinks about me I cannot imagine but I know very well what I think about him.

31
British Genius

Every year the Institute of Directors (which I joined shortly after the war) lays on a very formal lecture. The venue varies from year to year. The speakers do not conform to any particular pattern and have included the Governor of the Bank of England, the Duke of Kent, Mr. Peter Ustinov and myself.

I was invited to give the sixth annual lecture which I duly delivered on Tuesday, 2nd July, 1974, in Grosvenor House. The Chair was taken by Lord Pritchard (then Sir Derek Pritchard, Chairman of the Institute) under whom I had worked on the now defunct British National Export Council. The vote of thanks was proposed by Alan Lennox-Boyd (Lord Boyd of Merton), a lifelong friend.

Here follows the text of my lecture:–

I was naturally flattered when I was invited to deliver the annual lecture of our Institute. Disquiet, however, tempered my sense of gratitude when I was informed by Sir Richard Powell that the title "British Genius" had been assigned to the lecture.

Everyone has his own ideas about the meaning of the word genius but an examination of our country's affairs on the actual day upon which my invitation was received did not disclose to me anything that I myself had ever associated with the word genius.

Inflation was, of course, rampant. Four major unions were on strike and two universities in a state of open revolt. Northern Ireland was, as now, upon the brink of civil war. Our trade figures were disastrous. Half the country's petrol pumps were shut. The nation was working a 3-day week and many firms were discovering that they had in point of fact been working a 3-day week for some time past, but had been requiring 5 days in which to do it.

There was a grave shortage of milk bottles in our part of Gloucestershire, not to mention a national shortage of toilet paper. Indeed, the only example of genius that was readily apparent was our sustained skill in kicking the ball through our own goal.

Through the deepening darkness occasioned by the rationing of electricity in our office, I peered again at Sir Richard's instructions, to see whether there might not perhaps be a question mark at the end of the words "British Genius". Finding none, I decided that I had better go round to the Institute and clear the matter up with Sir Richard himself. I must find out from him what it was that had re-aroused his confidence in the state of our country's affairs. On arrival, however, at our Institute's HQ, I was informed that Sir Richard Powell had left that morning for Australia.

Uneasily I trudged back to my desk and there a consoling thought overtook me. Perhaps Sir Richard meant me to understand the word genius in a wider sense – not just the "special mental endowments" (I quote the Oxford English Dictionary) that are needed to write Hamlet, build St. Paul's, invent the steam engine and radar, or discover penicillin. Perhaps I was also to consider the "ethos, character, taste and spirit of a nation" – such as I suppose might be typified by the Monarchy, Government by consent, and the Rule of Law; Nelson, and Windsor Castle; and on a slightly different plane, Capability Brown, Pimms No. 1, the Edinburgh Tattoo, the T.U.C. and Eton.

Whatever interpretation we choose to put upon the word, no one can doubt that the British genius in all its aspects is at the moment sorely tried. We are obviously in trouble. The British, we are told (and too often tell ourselves) behave best when they have their backs to the wall. Possibly; but at the moment, too many of us refuse

180

to believe that our backs are anywhere near the wall. And if we eventually pull ourselves together and face the facts, we shall probably heave a sigh and say "It'll be all right on the night. We've been through all this before. Somehow we'll muddle through."

As a nation, we have a predilection for sackcloth and ashes. A Victorian Bishop of Gloucester, speaking in 1847 to a farmers' dinner in Cirencester near where I live, had these criticisms to level against the British genius. And his observations were duly reported in the *Wilts and Gloucestershire Standard* with which is incorporated (then as now) the *Swindon Express* and *Malmesbury Advertiser*.

The nation, said our Bishop, is in sorry disarray. The authority of the Church is in question. The law is in disrepute. Children turn aside from the guidance of their parents and their teachers. The labouring man has no loyalty to his master. Abroad, our name stands in low repute. The future of Ireland remains as troubled as ever.

After a good deal more lamentation on these not unfamiliar lines, the Bishop concluded with some sharp criticism of the Cirencester City Fathers for the confusion in the streets on market day.

I am only too sorry that the Bishop did not live long enough to witness the construction of the Cirencester by-pass which is due for completion next summer, 127 years after he had lodged his wholly justifiable protest.

I also draw some consolation from the fact that we are not the only people in trouble. "There is something not altogether displeasing to us," says Le Rochefaucauld, "in observing the misfortunes of others."

We have strikes but those of Italy last much longer. We have a minority government but many other countries have survived minority governments for years. Compared with the Dutch, our students are models of decorum. We have unemployment but the Canadian figures are significantly worse.

Our criminal statistics are trivial compared with those

of America. Our payments admittedly never balance but it is difficult to find any major nation whose payments do. Our pornography is a children's romp compared with that of the Danes. And when it comes to inside dealing, asset stripping and reverse take-over bids, the whizz kids of Tokyo make their opposite numbers in the City of London look a lot of bumbling amateurs.

The real trouble, however, is this. Other nations can afford these luxuries and we can't. Nor do I think that we can any longer afford one of our least pleasing national characteristics, the practice of crying stinking fish and loudly drawing attention to our own national shortcomings. We seem to have a positive genius for self-denigration. We call it knocking. The Germans talk about *die Miesmacher* – the alarmists – the ugly-makers. You hear them at every cocktail party. You read them in every glossy magazine. You watch them on every TV programme.

In the Institute we are neither ugly-makers, nor are we complaisant.

We are, of course, particularly concerned about our country's performance in the world's markets. We worry about our expertise in management, labour relations, salesmanship and all the other commercial weapons essential to a country that has to live by its export of brains and goods and services.

This wasn't always so. Time was, when commercial know-how was not part of our national ethos. Commerce was once a dirty word. Dr. Johnson thought that wool merchants were such beastly fellows that it was not even necessary to pay their bills.

When the first of Lord Carrington's line was introduced into the House of Lords, their Lordships marched out in a body because Lord Carrington was only a banker.

In one of the Palliser novels, a flunkey is reproved for ushering the Chairman of a brewery into the hall, instead of directing him to the Tradesmen's entrance.

Even so, Napoleon called us a nation of shopkeepers and it always annoys the French that the British have never been able to understand whether this was intended as a compliment or an insult.

We have moved a long way from Dr. Johnson and trade is no longer a dirty word. It may well be that one of the results of this turn around is that we over-react to our own performance.

But some of this self-criticism is, unfortunately, justified, particularly in the fields of delivery dates, technical finish and after-sales service. I think, nevertheless, we go too far in blazoning our mistakes, much to the comfort of our foreign competitors, some of whom have themselves, as we have discovered to our cost, deliberately, but secretly, promoted the first criticism.

We can, however, hardly be surprised if people take us, our goods, our services and our capabilities at our own valuation.

We have every right to be proud of our past achievements, even if a nostalgic worship of the past and too much respect for tradition is something to which our critics repeatedly point. But in the midst of our present anxieties, let us for a moment forget the genius of Shakespeare and Nelson and take comfort from our present achievements.

Our overseas investment is sixteen thousand million pounds, second only to that of the U.S.A. The know-how of the City of London, said *Time Magazine*, dwarfs all others.

The British Merchant Marine is the largest in the world.

We've won more Nobel Prizes for science than any country outside the U.S.A.

Our agricultural production is greater than that of Australia and New Zealand put together.

Of Europe's 200 biggest companies, 50% are British.

London is the centre of the world's art market.

Adlai Stevenson thought that London had the best public transport system of any city he knew.

The New York Chamber of Commerce thinks Marks & Spencers is the best run organisation of its kind in the world. So incidentally, does Marks & Spencers.

London is the only capital city where you can get a tooth stopped for free on a Sunday. In Peking you can get one pulled out but not stopped.

Half the Rolls Royces ever built are still on the road and running properly.

The British judge is the best judge in the world and a Cox's Orange Pippin the best apple.

Times are hard but there's hope for the old country yet.

So much for our successes. From time to time, we British are tempted to throw all our blunders into a heap and call them our bad luck. Equally, we have no right to attribute to our genius something which is really what the lawyers would call an Act of God. And although I'm a lawyer myself and not a theologian, I've always thought it a little unfair to put the blame so persistently on the Almighty for burst pipes, thunderbolts, gas leaks and Hurricane Betsy. Surely these may occasionally be called Acts of the Devil?

Consider, therefore, for a moment, the British weather. Even though it rivals sex as a topic of general conversation it's still, I think, rather unjustly maligned. Charles II argued in its defence that a man could be more usefully employed out of doors in England for more days of the year than in any other country in the world. And although one must beg leave to challenge Charles II as an authority on employment *out* of doors, he has here a point.

But where, of course, our genius has really lain is in our ability to turn our dull bland climate to good commercial advantage. Cotton and wool fibre, for instance, need damp to keep them supple. The wool weavers of Yorkshire and the cotton spinners of Lancashire soon discovered how to convert their wet weather into money.

In the countryside, a harsher climate would not have

helped Capability Brown who managed to turn the English garden into a national trade-mark.

Turnip Townshend and Coke of Norfolk discovered what controlled agriculture and properly planned grazing would do for British livestock. And all over the world, descendants of that livestock in pen, sty, byre, stable and starting gate bear witness to our genius for turning soft grass into hard cash.

Our soft grass and mild climate has enabled us to foster new sports. Racing, golf, football and particularly cricket – a game which the English, not being a spiritual people, have invented in order to give themselves some conception of eternity – all owe their development to our climate.

Our forebears always set great store by what they called the round man, the man of wide culture and varied skills who could turn his hand to anything. Voltaire was less polite about this paragon. Dilettante; Jack of all trades, he sneered, and master of none; typical of the British desire to get the best of all worlds, without actually earning it.

But we like the professional amateur and are beginning to suspect that the eager beaver doesn't always have the advantage over the talented all-rounder.

Down the years there have been many examples of the round man.

There are in particular two round Englishmen to whom even Voltaire's criticism could hardly be applied.

Henry VIII was the brightest Prince of our Renaissance, virile, statesmanlike, cultured, treacherous, unchaste; and he founded the Royal Navy. He also over-estimated his prowess as a wrestler. On the Field of the Cloth of Gold, he challenged François I to a bout and was soundly beaten. He was naturally furious and André Maurois always thought that the British distrust of foreigners in general and the French in particular sprang from that unfortunate hassel.

There was another round man who also had difficulties with the French.

He was a statesman, soldier, orator, painter, author, bricklayer and genius. Whether he was the greatest Englishman who ever lived is for future generations to decide but they may be guided by General de Gaulle who once magnanimously referred to Winston Churchill as "history's child". Indeed, I go further than round men. I also like to think that we are a round nation. A catalogue of our achievements would look extravagant, even smug. Something would inevitably be overlooked and somebody (inevitably Scots or Welsh) would protest.

There is, however, scarcely any field of human endeavour which the British have not entered and adorned.

Some of our genius may occasionally be too akin to accident for comfort. The Chinese discovered roast pork by burning down a pigsty and it took them quite a while to realise that it was not necessary to burn down a pigsty every time you fancied roast pork. Horace Walpole called this serendipity, the happy accident, but I believe that serendipity and genius cannot be far apart.

Take, for instance, the discovery of penicillin, gravity, the steam engine, radar and the jet; a formidable display of British genius. Chance was, of course, involved, but James Watt, Isaac Newton, Alexander Fleming, Robert Watson Watt and Frank Whittle were nevertheless men of real genius. They saw what everybody else had seen, but they then went away and thought what nobody else had thought. That's really what genius is about.

Just as the spectator sometimes sees most of the game, so the foreigner may sometimes be able to make a clearer assessment of our genius than we can ourselves. Not all foreigners, however, see us in the rosiest of lights.

The French, regrettably, think that we're perfidious and the fact that English is supplanting French as the language of diplomacy only serves to reinforce that opinion. Nevertheless, President Pompidou, shortly before he died, felt sufficiently mollified to declare that one of Britain's more acceptable tasks was to teach others how to live.

All the same, Erasmus, the Dutchman, complained that upon a visit to Cambridge he was beset by thieves, the bedbugs were the size of bears and the wine tasted like vinegar. He was staying, incidentally, at Trinity but I believe the situation has improved somewhat since Rab Butler became Master.

Ogden Nash thought that the British had a wonderful sense of humour but, unfortunately, nobody else understood it. Mark Twain, another perceptive critic, said that he would like to die in Manchester because the transition between Manchester and death would be almost unnoticeable.

On a visit to this country shortly before his death, Ben Gurion drew attention to the fact that in a technological age, 80% of senior British civil servants were still arts graduates. This fact, he said, was reflected in our whole attitude to scientific matters. If, for instance, anything went wrong with their computer, the British fell about with laughter, slapped their thighs and said they had always known that old Charlie could do it better on the back of an envelope. If a German computer went wrong, the Germans blanched and ran around like beetles on a hot plate until they had got it right.

A kindlier analysis of the British genius was once made by President Truman. Shortly after his retirement, he came down to Oxford to receive an honorary degree, and few men have deserved it more. Later that evening he dined in my own College, Christ Church, and after dinner he mused aloud upon our national characteristics.

They were largely unsensational, he said, and since they did not readily fire the imagination they easily slipped the memory, but they were, nevertheless, fundamental and formidable. A love of law and order and a respect for government by consent. A belief in honest administration. A dislike of hurting people and if a hurt be done a great effort to put it right. A tolerant people, offering a friendly hand to the victims of intolerance.

Skill in devising ways of improving the lot of mankind but a dreadful inability to follow those ideas through. A sweet countryside, he added, but appalling ways of cooking what that countryside produces. I don't actually remember how the cook at Christ Church reacted to that last observation though in support of President Truman's strictures, one must record that an Edwardian Dean once informed the Governing Body that the Almighty had removed Mr. Bultitude, the College cook, from their midst. "If he had not done so," the Dean added, "I should have been compelled to do it myself."

There are, of course, a variety of views about our behaviour in the kitchen.

I recently completed a ten year stint as President of the London Tourist Board and I used to keep a careful eye on our postbag. We received some letters of complaint, of course, but many more, I'm glad to say of commendation. The Mayor of Denver, Colorado, for instance, told us that in his opinion Britain's greatest contributions to modern civilisation were Laurence Olivier's Shylock and breakfast at the Connaught Hotel.

Not all our correspondents were so polite about our cooking and although it has obviously improved greatly in the last decade, I could not really assert that the word genius was very frequently associated in our mail with our cooking. Readers of the *Chicago Tribune*, for instance, were informed that a decent meal could be obtained almost anywhere in Britain as long as you stuck to French, Italian and Spanish restaurants.

Even this, however, was not quite so ambiguous as the *Canadian Travel News* which once described the Grand Hotel at Cromer as having hot and cold running water, English style.

Another sad gap in the roll call of our genius lies in the field of music. Despite our excellence as orchestral players and choral singers, we just do not produce really great composers.

I've often wondered why this should be because palpably, we are not Philistines. This failing was sometimes touched upon by my fellow students when I was studying music at Bonn University. (I think they meant it kindly, but with Germans you can never tell.) The composition class, for instance, used to confuse me by saying that my work would be known long after Beethoven's was forgotten, but not before. The other muses, however, have been on better terms with our genius, particularly in the fields of literature, architecture, painting and on the stage.

In literature we are rich beyond the dreams of avarice.

In the world of letters, Dr. Johnson accorded pride of place to Chaucer, Shakespeare and Milton. A century or so later, George Bernard Shaw gave pride of place to Chaucer, Shakespeare and himself. You pays your money and you takes your choice.

And what a choice it is. In short, the greatest literature in the world is English.

"Here's richness," said Mr. Squeers in *Nicholas Nickleby* and Dickens himself is pretty high up on the list. But in Shakespeare at least we have one supreme genius. Apart from his own dazzling gifts, Shakespeare enjoyed another tremendous advantage, a serendipity even. He, like the translators of the authorised version of the Bible, was writing in the English tongue just as it had blossomed into the richest, most expressive and most decorative language ever moulded by the lips of man. And, incidentally, our most valuable export.

Our paintbrushes, too, have not been ill-employed though we were, of course, late starters. We do not have a Dürer, a Leonardo or a Rembrandt. Indeed, apart from our miniaturists, we hardly started painting at all until the eighteenth century but then our genius went to work with a will.

Again, you must take your own choice. Mine is for Constable, Turner and a spectacular late starter, the quintessentially English George Stubbs. And in a minor key, the Norwich School; on their own merits and not just because most of them lived or worked in the parish of Mancroft from where I happen to come. But who could paint trees and skies like John Crome or draw churches like John Sell Cotman? But then, where do you find such trees and where did they build such churches?

Churches, yes. *Si monumentum requiris, circumspice,* but look a little further than St. Paul's and you will see in British architecture what is possibly the greatest of all our physical achievements.

We may not be brilliant cooks or great composers but we do build supremely well. Correction. We have hitherto built supremely well. The Great Fire of London, by a happy serendipity, gave room for the genius of Gibbs, Hawksmoor, Vanbrugh and Christopher Wren.

Hitler's blitz, less fortunately, gave room for up-ended glass and concrete beer crates, complete with rateable values and plot ratio. And it is interesting to note that the Australians have referred to their new opera house in Sydney Harbour as a monument of extravagance and unsuitability, despite the fact that it was not designed by Sir Basil Spence.

But go back a few years and look at Windsor Castle, Hatfield or St. Paul's. Look particularly at our smaller country houses, look at the chairs and clocks which Chippendale and Tompion put into them, look at our civic architecture, our town planning in Bath and Edinburgh, Belgravia and Regent's Park. Look at the way we have exported that architectural panache all over the world.

And what about our palaces? The success of our forefathers in wars, marriages and other such speculations enabled them to build more than their fair share of palaces. Horace Walpole said that the Mausoleum at Castle Howard was so splendid that it almost encouraged one to be buried alive. If you can get the Dean and Chapter to allow it, there are even grander places in which to be buried dead. Lincoln Cathedral, for instance; one of the finest Gothic buildings in the world, its great west front looking like a slap in the Devil's face. Not far behind are Canterbury and York, Ely, Wells and Salisbury. And remember, please, that those great churches were built with tools largely unchanged since the days of the Romans. The builders, however, rejoiced in one thing the Romans lacked. They built because they were inspired by a blinding faith in the love of Almighty God.

Unfortunately, the people who go into those cathedrals today are mostly tourists and more interested in time exposures than in evening prayer. I had this fact brought home to me once when a Japanese tour guide rang us up at the London Tourist Board and asked if St. Paul's was open on a Sunday.

I included the Edinburgh Tattoo amongst my original examples because pageantry forms such a significant part of our national ethos.

We like to think we do it pretty well but then, of course, we've been at it a long time. There was the first Prince of Wales at Caenarvon. The Barons at Runnymede. There was Elizabeth's bravura performance at Tilbury, when she demonstrated the basic purpose of Public Relations, namely to re-arrange the truth so that people will like you. Coronations, pageants, tournaments, tattoos, the Opening of Parliament, Trooping the Colour, you name it and the British can lay it on. Whether we don't lay it on a bit too thick is a different matter.

Why, ask the critics, does the British Tourist Authority go banging on about Bobbies and Beefeaters when we ought to be giving the world a picture of the new Britain – gritty, pragmatic, thrusting eagerly into a nuclear age; far removed from the Ceremony of the Keys and May Day on Magdalen Tower, Pratt's Club and the Eton Boating Song.

The trouble is that tourists don't come here to see the Atomic Power Stations at Harwell and Dounreay or take conducted tours around Guest, Keen & Nettlefolds. They come for our scenery, our history and pageantry.

191

They come to see Stratford on Avon, the Changing of the Guard and the backs at Cambridge; and they come in very large though no longer increasing numbers.

One of the many things upon which our visitors make favourable comment is the warmth of the welcome which we extend to them. The natives, in short, are friendly. Long may it stay that way. There was at one time a risk of that friendliness becoming strained by a feeling that the natives were being jostled off their own pavements and the life of their towns and cities brought to a standstill by too many tourists concentrated in too few places for too few days in the year.

You obviously won't make much profit in organising a package tour to Wolverhampton in mid-February but we must try and, indeed, I think, are succeeding in presenting a wider view of Britain to our visitors. And I think also that it's most important to maintain the distinction between a genuine tradition and a tourist gimmick.

The difference between a military ceremonial, such as the Trooping, and a theatrical display, such as the Tournament, is important.

To evaluate this difficulty, however, one has to remember the public dismay whenever some ceremonial has to be cancelled to allow the troops to go about their unenviable business on the battlefields of Londonderry and Belfast.

That distinguished German student of war, Von Clausewitz, once observed that not only were the British an unmilitary people but what was worse they didn't seem to think it mattered.

If by this he meant that we haven't gone through history looking for convenient wars to wage he was right. If he meant that the British soldier, sailor and airman has left no mark of his genius on history's roll of honour, then he is of course woefully wrong. Our armed forces have, in fact, made a much greater contribution than the country has ever deserved. "It's Tommy this and Tommy that and Tommy run away;

but thank you, Mr. Atkins, when the band begins to play."

Kipling, as usual, was right. Over the centuries we have consistently starved our armed forces of the men, money, materials and encouragement which they have needed to carry out their task. We then take it for granted that they will carry out that task with the utmost courage and skill. Fortunately for the country, they invariably do. Accidents have, of course, occurred. Admirals have run their ships into each other in broad daylight, elderly and unpractised cavalry generals have occasionally failed to understand quite simple messages. Worst of all, we have repeatedly mistaken a disaster for a triumph.

Indeed, Winston was forced to remind the country that Dunkirk was not a victory. Field Marshal Alexander put it even more concisely on the day before the final evacuation. He looked up and down the beaches and, turning to his slightly disgruntled staff, said, "Gentlemen, I cannot bring myself to believe that this campaign is going in our favour."

If it was this spirit that annoyed Von Clausewitz, then there is obviously much to commend it. As President Truman said, the British do not like hurting people. We are not a warlike race. But when we have had to take up arms we have done it with a courage, pertinacity and sheer professional skill which our critics either at home or abroad should not be allowed to forget.

Even so, Alex, himself the most professional of professionals, had to point out that we number amongst our commanders of genius, Clive of India, Oliver Cromwell and the Black Prince, none of whom had more than a smattering of professional training. I myself derive some comfort from this, because a Commanding Officer once reported on me that I was an officer whom the troops would follow anywhere, if only out of curiosity.

Genius is not only a matter of opinion, it is also a matter of taste. And just as one man's meat is another man's poison so what to me may be a fine example of the nation's ethos may to you be yet another example of our national gift of self-deception, and delusions of grandeur. Many of our most obvious characteristics are also amongst the most controversial. To some they bear witness to the Nation's genius for survival. To others they are symbols of a class-ridden and effete society. Take, for instance, the House of Lords.

The House of Lords is, I suppose, indefensible. For years we have tinkered with minor reforms until only some major reform would now make sense. But here we are faced with a paradox because any major reform must inevitably make the Lords less indefensible. But if you strengthen the defensibility of the Lords, you immediately increase its political vulnerability. With all its faults and they are painfully obvious, the Lords is still an effective brake upon dictatorship, though I should hate to see the brakes ever tested.

For that reason I myself am immensely proud to have been for nearly 32 years a member of the House of Lords even though it does owe so much of its success to the permanent absenteeism of 75% of its members. I would, however, hate to see the Lords abolished or pass into limbo.

And what of that peculiarly British institution, the Public School, which is, of course, not public at all but extremely private. Our present rate of taxation will probably close the lot. Nevertheless, parents who still believe they have the right to buy for their children the education they want, will apparently deny themselves almost anything in order to pay the enormous fees which the public schools are now forced to charge.

With all its faults, I think that a Public School education gives a boy two very real advantages. He is taught in a class which is small enough to give him some chance of individual attention. And at quite an early age a public school boy learns how to put up with injustice.

What else? The Police, the Royal Academy, fox hunting, the Honours List; there are plenty more examples of our national character and ethos which are sacrosanct to some and anathema to others.

None more so than the Monarchy itself. Now, the Monarchy is obviously vulnerable to attack from every angle. But as an integral part of our constitution it can boast two particularly British attributes – it suits us and it works. In a world increasingly subject to spasms of social and political lunacy we should realise how lucky we are to have at the centre of our affairs an institution of unchanging values.

Every weekend I drive past Windsor Castle on my way down to the Cotswolds. I give it more than a passing glance. To a militant monarchist such as myself, Windsor Castle is of special significance.

To me it presents a vastly impressive image of strength and authority, of the melding of sovereign and subject; of emergent monarchy and nation state. To me it signifies the power that long ago brought peace – the King's peace to a divided and belligerent society.

All over Europe the kings have departed. They have left the palace-monastery of the Escorial; the Emperors have gone from the Hofburg and Schönbrunn, from the Kremlin and the Winter Palace. The Louvre and Versailles are museums, the Tuileries no more; Sans Souçi and Hradschin are under the Communist heel. Windsor alone continues to fulfil the functions for which it was originally intended. To me the panoply of the annual Garter ceremony in St. George's Chapel appears as the embodiment of service; service within the bounds of Church and State. And service, at all levels, is something which today is in very short supply.

And more. For me the castle stands for the sense of national continuity allied to our ability to compromise, the willingness to accept change which runs throughout our history. It has seen the emphasis move from the dictatorship of the Normans and Plantagenets to the modern concept of the Rule of Law and Government by consent.

These two basic concepts of our constitution and thus

of our freedom have been carried by the British all round the world. America and the old dominions have retained them almost intact. Other parts of our former Empire have not, admittedly, found the Westminster model to their taste and have rejected it. To take only one dreadful example; the International Commission of Jurists has recently reported that in Uganda there has been a total breakdown of the rule of law. And although General Amin assures us that Uganda still enjoys freedom of speech one cannot help but ask how much freedom there still is after the speech.

Dean Acheson said that Britain had lost an Empire and not yet found a role. The jibe was too near the truth for comfort. We did not, as a matter of fact, lose an Empire. We transferred it and despite the growing pains, we have left an enormous amount of goodwill behind us. We have also left a lasting memorial to the genius of the ordinary men and women who built it.

This memorial will not vanish overnight. And what is more, I believe that history will eventually give us much greater credit for our imperial achievements than Dean Acheson and his fellow Americans were prepared to acknowledge. Indeed, they hastened our departure. On the other hand, we shall not overnight settle down to our new role as a European rather than a world power. The political problems involved are difficult enough in all conscience. To make matters worse we are attempting to do this at a time when, for our Western neighbours as well as ourselves, absolute standards are under greater pressure than at any time in modern history.

Crime, violence, corruption, racial tension and atheism are commonplace. None of these problems are peculiar to this country and none of our neighbours are better at finding a solution than we are.

To the serious social problems which face nearly all the Western world we have to add another and even greater problem peculiar to ourselves. Two of the most outstanding of our national characteristics – the rule of law and government by consent – are not only under attack in our former colonial possessions; they are now under attack here at home and because the attack is less obvious and less easily recognised it is all the more dangerous. Too often we hear the question, who really rules the country – Parliament or the Trade Unions?

Reluctance to face a threat usually implies a lack of confidence. A crisis of confidence is as much as anything a crisis of leadership. We know well enough that there are no bad soldiers, only bad officers. We also know that Churchills and Wellingtons and Nelsons and Disraelis do not grow on trees. Leadership is a hall-mark of the British character and it has often been found at its best and its most inspired amongst quite ordinary men and women. It is today too often a commodity for which we look to somebody else to provide. Too many people, when invited to stop belly-aching and give a little leadership, cross over the road and look the other way. Too many people, whose voices ought to be heard, just cannot bother to stand up and be counted.

Who are these people? Politicians, perhaps? Politics are, unfortunately, in disrepute. The authority of Parliament is passing from Westminster to Whitehall. Parliamentary Government has not yet become Presidential government, but the time may not be far off. But if something is wrong with Parliamentary democracy, then the place to put it right is in Parliament itself.

In the forties and fifties, the flow of new recruits into Parliament and into local government was impressive both in quality and quantity. Now too many of tomorrow's potential leaders just do not want to know. There is a dearth of highclass Parliamentary candidates and far too many highclass retirements.

Today, the letters M.P. after your name are beginning to lose their attraction for the sort of people who should be leading the country tomorrow.

So are the letters J.P., except for those who want them for the wrong reason. So is the humble but important word, Councillor, before your name. The best way to drive corruption out of local government is not to worry so much about declarations of interests but to get better men and women into local government. And those who, understandably enough, think that there is too much party politics in local government might ponder on affairs in Newcastle where not enough party politics resulted in one party dictatorship. People in this country are still judged not only by the company they keep, but by the company they keep away from. And that also goes for business in general and the City of London in particular.

There are more able and good men at work in the City than ever and despite one or two recent displays that should never have been allowed to happen, the City's reputation remains as high as ever.

But in commerce and industry again there is a shortage of men and women who are prepared to step outside their factory or office and give a lead in wider fields. Firms cannot or will not spare good people to run for office, to serve on professional and national bodies; to broadcast; to lecture; to flatter, cajole and persuade.

Accordingly, the case of reasoned moderation too often goes by default.

The same applies in even greater force to the Trade Unions and there, a reluctance of the more sober rank and file to take a proper part in a Union's affairs has had disastrous repercussions. Mr. Hugh Scanlon, after all, was elected to power by less than 10 per cent of his membership.

There are many aspects of leadership. To opt out should not be one of them. We can't all be commanders-in-chief but need so many be content as camp followers?

Hitler, of all people, gave a good recipe for a country's greatness. It depended, he said, upon that country's natural genius, upon the proper development of its raw materials and upon hard work. I have already offered some comments upon the subject of genius. Of our raw materials, the oldest is brains and the newest North Sea Oil. I know nothing about North Sea Oil. Indeed, my knowledge of North Sea Oil could be put into a nutshell whilst still leaving ample room for the nut. I trust, therefore, that our leaders have not falsely raised my hopes.

Nor, unfortunately, do I know how to make a man work. I do, however, know how to discourage the very man to whom I suggest we should be looking for leadership. To tell a man that if he works hard, makes use of his brains and succeeds at his task, he will be taxed until he howls with anguish won't encourage him to work harder. Nor will it encourage his faith in the principles of government by consent. I do not find there any of the give and take, any of the feeling of compromise upon which all democratic government must be based. That is, in fact, government by envy, hatred and malice and it is unworthy of a great country.

Everybody is in favour of social justice. The rich must, of course, pay taxes at a higher rate than the poor, but don't let anyone deceive himself that you can make the poor richer by making the rich poorer. The purpose of taxation is to raise revenue, not to pay off old political scores. Present policies, if carried much further, will make industry unmanageable and, eventually, the country ungovernable.

We are, indeed, in grave difficulties. We face both a constitutional and a financial crisis and too many people just do not want to know. I myself, however, will not believe the *Miesmachers*, the ugly makers. I do not believe that a country such as this can lose its touch or play itself out. I just will not believe that after all we've endured and achieved in the last thousand years our genius will desert us; that a nation such as this will fail to find leadership, will turn its face to the wall and give up. I simply will not believe that we have come to the end of our political, commercial and spiritual resources.

Amongst my first examples of genius I mentioned, I think, the Nelson touch. Nelson was himself a fine example of British genius. He was brave, loyal, and kind, ever anxious for the wellbeing of his men and formidably professional. He was also a bit of a bounder, with that disregard for chastity which seems inseparable from the best of British genius.

Now, every schoolboy remembers Nelson's signal at Trafalgar. "England expects that every man this day will do his duty", but not everyone remembers Admiral Lord Collingwood's reply when he received it. He turned to his Flag Lieutenant on the deck of H.M.S. *Royal Sovereign* and remarked rather testily, "I wish to God Nelson would stop sending us these damn fool signals. We all realise perfectly well what we have to do today." I wish, to God, Mr. Chairman, *we* all realised perfectly well what *we* have to do today.

32

Stop the Clock – We've made too much Progress

A short while after I had addressed the Institute of Directors in London, I received an invitation from Sir Robert Crichton-Brown, the President of the Institute of Directors in Australia, to address their own Sixth National Conference in Sydney.

My arm needed no twisting.

In due course, Sir Robert greeted me on the steps of the Wentworth Hotel. There was a large crowd milling around the hotel doors and I told Sir Robert that, grateful though I was, he need not have laid on quite such a big welcoming party. Sir Robert explained apologetically that the party had not actually come to welcome me. They had come to boo Mr. Nelson Rockefeller who was due to address a political gathering in the hotel that evening.

My morale was restored, however, when I cast my eye over the list of other speakers with whom I was to share the next day's platform. They included the Governor-General (Sir John Kerr), his successor, Sir Zelman Cowen (then Vice-Chancellor of Queensland University), the Prime Minister (Rt. Hon. Malcolm Fraser) and a popular stand-up music-hall comedian named Paul Hogan who addressed us in a dialect known as Ocker. This, I should explain, sounds like a cross between Cockney and Gaelic and I'm afraid I didn't quite grasp everything he was saying. Mr. Hogan explained to me afterwards, however, that he was being rude at the expense of Mrs. Gough Whitlam, the wife of the former Prime Minister, who had recently been sacked, amidst some tumult, by the Governor-General. Mr. Hogan then added that he had not understood a single word of what I had said either, so honours were even.

Here follows the text of what he had failed to understand, delivered in Syndey on the 1st April 1976.

Whilst I was thinking about a subject that might be acceptable to you today, two very different things happened which, on reflection, had something in common. First, the Concorde made its first commercial flight. Now, I know all about the Concorde. It lives in the next village to us at Fairford in Gloucestershire.

On most Sunday mornings it takes off at about six o'clock, flies through our bedroom window, down past the bathroom and out over the coalshed towards the Bristol Channel.

I don't think it makes much more noise than any other aircraft although we all know that a golden statue awaits the man who can invent a silent jet. Apart from that, it is extremely good-looking; I think it's a wonderful technical achievement. I, personally, am very proud of it, and I am grieved that it has run into such bad luck.

For me, however, the acme of travel luxury would be that demanded by Sir Joshua Camps who refused to accompany Captain Cook on his second voyage to Australia unless he could have not one but two horn players to entertain him during dinner.

The other thing that happened was very different and that was the death of General Franco. You will remember the poor man's ordeal, operation after operation. You may also have remembered that little poem: *"Thou shalt not kill yet need not strive officiously to keep alive"*.

I am not therefore surprised at the number of people who tell their doctors and their families that they do not wish to end their lives as cabbages, in order to bear witness to medical skill and ingenuity.

This seems to be a different sort of progress, a case

where the pendulum of the clock has swung too far in the opposite direction and it is on this subject that I would like to offer a few observations and suggest a few ways in which we might put things to rights.

Of course, there are several basic concepts about what the word progress really means. The Oxford English Dictionary gives us "Forward or onward movements, advance, development". All right – but some of these are highly arguable definitions. The only example that I can really think of where "forward and onward movement" is self-evident is that of the Gadarene Swine.

I'm afraid that too many of us are joining their ranks in the name of progress. I also think that far too much of what we rather glibly call progress is really nothing of the sort.

It is simply one more lurch towards the Gadarene cliff and I am beginning to fear that in the name of progress we are in danger of losing too many of the few remaining decencies of life. It isn't really progress if a cannibal starts to use a knife and fork.

Now, of course, I'm not suggesting that we should abolish the telephone, the jet, space-travel, penicillin, sliced-bread and the computer.

Well, half a minute; I'm not at all certain about the computer and apologise to any computer manufacturers who may be members of the Institute. I do, however, remember when the Governing Body of All Souls first installed a computer at their college in Oxford. The savants, the scholars and the Divines all gathered eagerly around. "Let us now test this machine to the uttermost," they said. So, into the appropriate slot they inserted a piece of paper bearing the awe-inspiring question, "Is there a God?" From the other end there immediately emerged the answer, "There is now".

Perhaps I am worrying unduly about computers but it so happens that our local electricity company has written several times to apologise that although my quarterly account is obviously in error, there's nothing they can do about it until the Spring as my bill is already in the computer and cannot be extracted. I suspect this sort of progress is occurring the world over.

Could we not, therefore, occasionally try and turn the clock back? Have we not, here and there, made too much progress? And do not let us shrug our shoulders hopelessly and say that it's all gone too far. What can we poor mortals do?

Well, it so happens that the world over, men and women of goodwill are beginning to discover that there are plenty of things that can be done and they are beginning to push the clock gently back in the name of progress.

After all, every great reform must have started off as somebody's private opinion.

Consider for a moment what are now called the Amenities. The war did enough damage physically in all conscience without us trying to make it worse in the name of progress. The European Heritage Movement, for instance, has achieved a great deal in preventing the destruction of yet more fine buildings. Local amenity societies are springing up everywhere striving to preserve some local heritage.

However, you've got to be reasonable about preservation. You can put too big a spanner in the developer's works and make the Amenity Lobby look ridiculous. Even moderation can be carried to excess.

New roads just have to be built. Occasionally a fine view just has to be sacrificed for the sake of an essential new power station and sometimes the best can be the enemy of the good. The important thing is, however, that people are beginning to discover the damage that can be done in the name of progress, when they aren't paying proper attention.

A splendid British example is near the M23 London-to-Brighton Motorway, where they've built seven miles of lovely new road which actually goes from nowhere to nowhere.

I suppose that it is in the world of transport that the concept of progress is most suspect. I've already mentioned the Concorde. There is, however, another and more awkward side to the transportation story.

I don't know how long it is since you last dined at our Institute's headquarters in Belgrave Square. You would have dined, I hope, very well; but as you walked home across the Square, which is still one of the handsomest bits of town planning in Europe, you would have noticed a dozen vast lorries, most of which would have come across the Channel from Europe, and use Belgrave Square as their nightly roosting ground.

I observed that one of them had written on its tail board in several languages, "This lorry stops for traffic lights, level crossings and blondes. For red-heads it will back up 50 yards."

The driver, however, spoke little English nor could he translate the metric dimensions of the height, width and weight of his juggernaut into the dimensions of the small English roads and bridges over which he would undoubtedly have to pass.

This sort of thing is happening all over Europe. The European Heritage Movement has produced some horrifying examples of huge lorries crashing through the streets of handsome little medieval towns, knocking old bridges to pieces and ploughing ancient market places into ruins.

I myself remember once seeing a vast articulated monster jammed tight in the back streets of Cirencester, near where I live. I got out to remonstrate with the gentleman at the wheel. Just in time, I noticed that the lorry belonged to the Cunard Line, of which I was then managing director, so I got back quietly into my car and drove away.

Fortunately, public opinion in Europe is swinging to the view that this method of transporting heavy goods can hardly be described as progress. Long distance rail transport, despite considerable opposition from the unions, seems to be coming back into its own. Canals are being re-opened and redeveloped all over Europe. (This, by the way, will not only help to ease the traffic;

it will, I understand, also help to increase the population. It seems it's not easy to dodge in a barge.)

A large number of towns in Europe are now banned to all heavy lorries. Ring roads are being widened, by-passes constructed and bridges reinforced. I'm proud to say that in Britain we have frequently led the way, though one cannot, of course, overlook the fact that many British lorries are probably doing equal harm to French and Belgian cathedrals because, in spite of what you may have read about the plight of the British motor industry, the export of lorries from Britain is now the biggest in Europe. I can only hope the manufacturers' consciences are of the same proportion as their order books.

I am not one of those who travel thousands of miles for the privilege of abusing his own country or, indeed, even his own country's government, whatever views he may hold about it in the stilly watches of the night. Of necessity, however, these few examples of where I think the pendulum has swung too far must be drawn from my own experience. But I suspect that they may not be unfamiliar in some other countries as well.

A few weeks ago I took a pair of favourite shoes into Cirencester to be repaired. "Oh, no, sir", said the Pakistani gentleman in charge. "Not worth it at all. Pray dispose of them at once and purchase a new pair."

The same principle applies to watches and electrical appliances. It is also very difficult to get a roof thatched or a book bound, a tyre changed, a picture framed or a weathercock repaired.

Almost the rarest commodity today is a first-class shorthand typist. The job simply takes too long for the modern young person to learn. Incidentally, we now have to say "young person" in Britain since the passing of our new Sex Discrimination Act. You may no longer specify lady or gentleman when you advertise for a secretary and a barmaid is now called a bar person. Sex change operations are now called "gender re-assignments".

Even though I got married before the Act was passed I'm lucky to have a wife to tell me what to do and a secretary to do it.

In short, the progress of technocracy has turned a pair of human hands into a most expensive item of equipment. What, however, I am also seeking to argue is that although habits can be changed, a groove, once you're in it, is a very difficult thing to get out of and, sometimes, even the most beneficent form of progress can be self-defeating.

In Britain, as here, traffic still keeps to the left. For us Europeans to change over to the more widely accepted habit of driving on the right would be both progressive and sensible. We've decided, however, that the operation would be so expensive and so confusing that it just wouldn't be worthwhile. Heaven knows, decimal coinage has given us enough trouble. The traffic change would be ten times worse. Moral: don't be afraid of resisting even the most desirable piece of progress if the game just wouldn't be worth the candle.

They recently decided, incidentally, on this traffic change in India where there are slightly fewer cars and traffic lights than in Britain; but the bullocks wouldn't change their habits and the whole scheme had to be abandoned. Sensible chaps, bullocks. They should be given votes.

Now here's another example of reverse progress. I know that the subject of beer doesn't have a soothing effect on Anglo-Australian relations but you may be interested to learn that there is a strong and effective movement at home for a return to beer brewed and served in the old-fashioned way rather than the icy, gassy nothing which British brewers have been foisting upon us in the name of progress. But Lord help the Government department that may have to make us drink in litres rather than in pints.

We are also demanding a return to free-range eggs on the pernickety grounds that battery-produced eggs, though very scientific, do not actually taste like eggs.

What else? Well, it is beginning to dawn on most civilised countries that the destruction of rare and beautiful animals in the name of sport hardly constitutes progress and the power of public reaction is becoming impressive.

These are only a few random examples of what can be achieved if you keep your wits about you. But if you let your conscience wander for a moment, you can bet your boots that somebody will come along and pull your cathedral down to make room for a sewage works, fill your trout stream with commercial detergent or try to abolish the House of Lords.

And I'm not only talking about individual reactions to an individual dilemma. There are times when whole countries have learned to react to a sudden threat. Take, for instance, the reaction of Norway to the development of North Sea Oil, potentially a source of immense wealth.

In Norway, although farming, fishing and certain other industries have become increasingly "uneconomic", the Norwegians are happy to subsidise them in order to keep the remoter parts of the countryside populated and to preserve their particular way of life. It was because the Norwegians feared that the rules of the Common Market would destroy these traditional activities and patterns that they voted against it. They are deeply worried about the impact of North Sea Oil.

In Scotland, although local communities in the Shetlands, the Orkneys and elsewhere are equally worried about the breakup of their life, the Government, from financial necessity, has to regard this as expendable and is pressing on with production of the oil in spite of the social consequences. And the attitude of these island communities isn't just based on ignorance and backwardness. Most of those who live there have been, at one time or another, in centres of so-called "modern life" and have consciously rejected it, realising that a strong community with simple tastes has something to offer which compensates for the material difficulties.

The example of Norway, therefore, shows that governments can set the clock back, even if they seldom can afford to do so.

I suppose that one of the strongest links that binds both the countries of the Common Market and the English-speaking nations is respect for the rule of law. As a lawyer myself, it's perhaps pardonable that I should subscribe to this doctrine although I am beginning to suspect that when it comes to the rule of law, progress may possibly have overtaken justice.

In days gone by, if a man had a row with his neighbour, he shook his fist in his face and said, "I'll have the law on you." He doesn't do that so readily now. All too well, he knows the cost and time involved. What was once a bastion of our liberties is now regarded by too many people as a pot-hole to be avoided at all costs.

It would, of course, be an impertinence on my part to associate any of these sentiments with the legal situation in Australia but I have to bear witness that in one or two other Western countries where my business takes me, a disturbing number of people have come to regard the law as an enemy rather than a friend.

This ought to worry not only lawyers but also politicians, journalists and ordinary human beings since respect for the law goes to the heart of any democratic society. Yet, at a time when terrorism, hi-jacking, vandalism, drug-addiction, pornography and the glib rhetoric of dissent are all chipping away at our most hallowed institutions and any successful defence of them must rest on public esteem, those institutions that are particularly based on the English Common Law at present enjoy all too little public esteem.

So much is this true in Britain that the Government has had to set up a Royal Commission to examine the whole of our legal system. I'm afraid that this announcement comes not a minute too soon, although, according to the normal habits of Royal Commissions, its decisions will arrive several years too late and will inevitably cancel each other out.

But why is the law so unpopular? And why are lawyers equally unpopular until, of course, they become judges, when they are naturally sacrosanct.

I believe the reason may be this: the operation of most Western legal systems is slow and susceptible of the most shameless delaying tactics which frequently deter decent people from seeking their rights. Most of these systems are expensive to a degree which, again, deters the aggrieved litigant. In Britain, for instance, the legal aid system, though it obviously has much to commend it, is regarded as a pernickety burden on the taxpayer and a boon to the barrack-room lawyer.

To many people all legal systems this side of the Iron Curtain seem to be uncertain and capricious in their outcome.

Resort to the courts is a costly lottery, providing intellectual stimulus and enjoyment to practitioners of the law, but leaving the unfortunate litigant feeling as if he has been trapped in an uncontrollable machine. (This, of course, is the reason why so few lawyers themselves ever go to law.)

Most British lawyers and, I am sure, all Australian lawyers, will regard this criticism as unfair. They will feel that many of the matters of which I have been complaining are inevitable. They are the fault of an over-burdened legislature, or the perversity of events or even of human nature itself: particularly, of course, the nature of the other chap. But they hardly count as progress.

From time to time I write for a magazine called *Punch* and the editor recently published a cartoon showing an ashen-faced scientist emerging from a room marked "Think Tank" and clutching in his arms a sheaf of computer tapes. He was shouting anxiously to his friends, "Run for the hills". As I can well imagine what some of those tapes must have contained, I am almost tempted to have given these few remarks of mine a sub-title: "How to avoid the future". Unfortunately, however, I don't know any of the answers.

I do not know, for instance, how to cure unemployment. Nor do I know how to check inflation. Even our former Prime Minister, Mr. Harold Wilson, never claimed that he knew how to do this and Mr. Wilson is a very clever man, as he himself would be the first to admit.

I do not know how we can persuade people to go back to Church. I continue to be puzzled about education. Why is it that the more a country spends on education the more vigorously do students reject its benefits and set about tearing down their classrooms and setting fire to the Dean?

Is it really progress, I wonder to myself, to continue to spend so much money trying to educate the uneducable even though a man can only be regarded as uneducable when he can no longer listen to anything without losing his temper or his self-confidence.

More important still, I do not know how we can pick our way through the dangerous battlefields of management and organised labour, a battle in which most industrial nations are becoming increasingly involved.

In 1974, Ted Heath challenged the coalminers to say who should run the country, the Government or the miners, and he lost. He should have remembered that it is a rash man who takes on the Vatican, the Brigade of Guards or the National Union of Mineworkers.

Since then, the most powerful of the British Trade Union leaders have made it clear that having rejected a Conservative Government and secured an administration subservient to them, they propose to keep it that way.

The situation is not confined to Britain and I would not discuss it if it were. But let us suppose that at the next election in any European country a right-wing majority is returned. As soon as a suitable excuse can be found, massive strikes are called.

Suppose in short, that organised labour, on balance, simply refuses to accept the decision of the electorate. What then?

Such a situation, indeed, is already developing in Italy

and may arise later, possibly in France. Neither country is surer of the way out than we are in Britain. There are also pretty obvious signs that the Trade Unions of the other Common Market countries are combining with the same purpose in mind.

What, of course, gives the unions the power to act in this way is something quite fundamental. It is the fact that the more technical a society grows, the more vulnerable it is to disruption. This was not the concept of progress that James Watt had in mind when he invented the steam engine or Arkwright when he built the first spinning Jenny.

Conversely, progressive young men do not join the Loamshire Fusiliers in order to man power stations if the electricians go on strike.

The major problems that face Western Civilisation are all too painfully familiar – nuclear confrontation, the Third World, East and West, starvation and over-population, and the return to barbarism in countries where some of us thought we British had planted the seeds of civilisation.

Indeed, I believe that those of us with rather hazy ideas of freedom, democracy, equality of opportunity, which we have perhaps taken a little too much for granted, are beginning to realise that we may have posed ourselves more questions than we are really able to answer.

I have not ventured to touch on many of these major questions but only on a few of the consequential problems which I feel may go by default unless they are noticed in time.

Noticed in time – that I think is the essence of what I am trying to say. Not rejected in time, but noticed, examined and accurately assessed. For this we need diligence and a sense of values. That great American statesman Thomas Jefferson reminded us that the price of liberty is eternal vigilance. He also kept quite a number of slaves which to my way of thinking, detracts a little from the value of his views on liberty and possibly of his views of liberators.

If there's one thing worse than a tyrant, said Palmerston, it's a liberator. Louis XVI and the Tsar were both called tyrants by the two men who alledgedly liberated their fellow-citizens from tyranny. Their names were Robespierre and Stalin. Idi Amin of Ghana has also, in his time, referred to himself as a liberator.

This is what makes me, as you will by now have gathered, believe that our concepts of progress may have to change from time to time.

All change, said the Duke of Cambridge, with his usual military precision, should be resisted until it becomes irresistible. Change and progress are not quite the same thing and I do not therefore go all the way with His Grace. I would not, as I have said, do away with penicillin. Nor would I stop the clock long enough to ban the bicycle – probably the most harmless and beneficial invention ever bestowed upon mankind. But I would, however, try to preserve a sense of proportion whenever progress is proclaimed.

We live in an Orwellian age of double-speak. When revolution breaks out in some Banana republic and the Progressive Party comes up 99% victorious at the polls, you can be sure that a free Press will be shut down overnight in the name of progress; the Chief Justice will be shot and the Opposition thrown in gaol.

Progress and the right to stop the clock is also a matter of personal prejudice. Some while ago, the Tate Gallery in London laid a pile of bricks on the floor and the pile was highly praised in the media as a fine example of progressive art. I ventured to differ from this point of view and referred to the bricks in a debate on the BBC in derogatory terms. I was violently attacked for so doing, though not, I'm glad to say, by anybody whose opinion I valued.

That's the trouble. The progressives have all the vocal advantage and we poor old conservatives are nervous of speaking up, lest we be abused as unprogressive reactionaries.

So be it. I prefer Turner, Gainsborough and Stubbs to a load of old bricks, and I'm not afraid to ask that this particular clock be turned unashamedly back. Some weeks ago the Music Critic of the left wing London weekly, the *New Statesman*, praised a new composer for his courage in ridding himself of "the Shackles of the Tunesmith". This is yet another progressive move which I can do without. Beethoven, Bach and Schubert all wrote tunes and thundering good ones, too. I'm sure however, that our unshackled composers' work will be remembered long after theirs are forgotten, but not before.

If, when my time comes, the trumpets can be persuaded to sound for me on the other side, perhaps it could be Vivaldi's *Double Trumpet Concerto in C major* (a very unprogressive work), but if I have missed my way and am thundering along uninterrupted amongst the Gadarene swine, then please, will somebody, seize me by the tail and turn me progressively backwards.